Walter Chalmers Smith

North Country Folk Poems

Walter Chalmers Smith

North Country Folk Poems

ISBN/EAN: 9783744774260

Printed in Europe, USA, Canada, Australia, Japan

Cover: Foto ©Thomas Meinert / pixelio.de

More available books at **www.hansebooks.com**

HISTORIC LAYS,

AND

MINOR POEMS.

BY

[H]ILIP SMITH SPARLING.

"VOX ET PRÆTEREA NIHIL."

London:

GEORGE PHIPPS,

RANELAGH STREET, EATON SQUARE.

1851.

TO THE

REV. THOMAS UMFREVILLE STONEY, M.A.,

PERPETUAL CURATE OF PATELY, IN YORKSHIRE,

AS A REMEMBRANCE OF LOVED ONES GONE, WITH WHOM HIS

NAME IS EVER ASSOCIATED;

AND ALSO

AS A SMALL TRIBUTE OF THANKFUL ACKNOWLEDGMENT FOR

THE INSTILMENT OF THOSE PRINCIPLES WHICH

CAN ALONE GUIDE AND SUPPORT THE WAY-

FARER IN HIS JOURNEY THROUGH A

CHANGEFUL WORLD,

THIS LITTLE VOLUME

IS AFFECTIONATELY, YET MOST RESPECTFULLY, DEDICATED BY

HIS FORMER PUPIL AND EARLY FRIEND,

THE AUTHOR.

PREFACE.

IT is now some twelve years since I published
a little Volume of Original Poetry, under the
title of " A WREATH OF MINSTRELSIE." I said
in my Preface to that Book, that I did not present
myself in public with any conceit that I should
obtain rank or distinction as a Poet. One of the
long established periodicals of the then and present day, however, condescended to notice my
effusions in a much kindlier spirit than I ex-
pected; and, notwithstanding that a fastidious
acquaintance said, I' was ♦ damned with faint
praise," I congratulated myself on having been
paid several compliments. The Editor of the
periodical in question said I had an ear for music ;
but that which I considered the truer compliment,
was a remark, that I had formed a singularly
just appreciation of the merits of my own per-
formance.

I scarcely know what excuse to offer for appear-
ing a second time in print ; and all that I can say
is, that many who were permitted to read my
MSS., were, or seemed to be, pleased; and I

naturally perhaps, thought that others not disposed to be over critical, might also be similarly entertained.

It may be proper to add, that the "Battle of Crecy," and one or two of the minor Poems, have been already in print.

It is not the fashion of the present time to dispraise oneself, and to do so may seem like affectation; but for truth's sake, I feel compelled to remark, that the subjects chosen have not had ample justice done them by me. The faults and imperfections in the Work will be found to abound, and it is not unlikely there may be some plagiarisms; but with regard to these last, I trust I shall have credit when I say, that if there are any, they are wholly unintentional on my part.

COLCHESTER,
January 1851.

CONTENTS.

Historic Lays.

	PAGE
THE SETTLEMENT OF THE NORMANS	1
THE DEATH OF EDWARD THE MARTYR	35
THE ESCAPE OF PRINCE EDWARD	71
THE BATTLE OF CRECY	109
CHARLES II	131

Minor Poems.

RUNNIMEDE	149
QUEEN ELIZABETH AT TILBURY FORT	152
YOUNG ENGLAND	156
BERECHURCH	159
WALTON LE SOKEN	162
A RAMBLE	166
THE BEGINNING OF SORROWS	170
THE FALL OF ADAM	174
NURSERY RHYMES	179
TWELVE SONNETS	180
HENRI V	192
"HO! EVERY ONE THAT THIRSTETH"	193
THE TEARS OF LIFE GROW COLD	194
TO A THRUSH SINGING ON NEW YEAR'S DAY	196
IN M. M. M.	198
SONG	200
"THE END IS NOT YET"	202
"UPON THE EARTH DISTRESS OF NATIONS"	203

The Settlement of the Normans.

B

In the following sketch, I have drawn a little upon the imagination; but the chief incidents will be familiar to all who are conversant with Anglo-Saxon or French History. The style which I have adopted may appear somewhat rough and irregular; but perhaps it will not be found altogether unsuitable to the times and the personages, whose characters are intended to be represented; the ludicrous accident related in the end gave the tone to the piece.

The Settlement of the Normans.

———◆———

I.

UPROSE Jarl Rollo hastily;
   There's anger in his heart;
All marked it in his kindling eye;
And some who thought a fray was nigh,
   Were prest to take their part.
Down the brimful cup he flung,
Against his iron feet it rung.
Full wrathfully the Sea King spoke:
" I wot this revel thou hast broke;
   Not all would think it meet
To dare a Norseman who may claim,
For rank in arms and ancient name,
   The first in all thy fleet.

I care not for thy vassals here;
   But say in presence of each one,
To my good father's sword and spear
   Thou owest crown and throne:
But thankless thou hast ever been
   For all thy bold and lofty mien.
Who saved thy life on Storna's plain,
When left amongst the weltering slain,
I find thou hast all soon forgot.
I claim a boon, it matters not,
   Were it thy daughter's hand,
No better match will be her lot
   If you search throughout your land:
Take heed thou dost not rue the hour
   And wish thy words unspoken;
No man who braves the Rollo's power,
   Escapes without his token."

II.

Right heartily King Harfhold laughed
   His liegeman's rage to see :

He filled another cup, and quaffed
    The wine with right good glee :
" Now by my royal father's crown,
    Thou surely art too bold ;
I tremble much to see thy frown;
Come, nobles, let us all kneel down,
    Lest he begin to scold—
But mark, Sir Thane, should'st thou be found
    (We'll give thee grace to start)
On any part of Danish ground,
When three more suns have had their round,
    Thy head and shoulders part:
Now cool thy wrath, and if thou wilt,
    Eke out the night with us ;
Tho' good wine thou hast rashly spilt,
    We will not make a fuss."

III.

Rollo, who lov'd a roving life,
    Reck'd little such decree,
For ever 'midst the wild waves strife
    The more at home felt he.

Seldom his voice was heard to sound
   Within his castle-walls,
Save when the long Yule nights came round,
   And rose the Northern squalls;
If homeward then the Sea-King came
   With many a daring rover,
They thought the hours were dull and tame,
As they sat beside the midnight flame,
   Talking their past deeds over;
And when his banner was unrolled,
   His vassals tried and true,
All warriors of iron mould,
   Would follow him he knew:
So he closed the casque upon his head,
   And slight obeisance showing,
Strode from the hall with haughty tread,
   To watch the red stars glowing;
Venus and Mars such lustre shed,
And smiled so kindly o'er his head,
   The night-winds breathing sweetly,
That Rollo scarce was in his bed,
   Ere his rage was soothed completely.

IV.

All glorious is the summer day ;
  Two hundred sail and more, .
Are anchored in the rocky bay,
  Or riding near the shore ;
Banners are streaming in the breath
Of the light gale which wantonneth
  The merry waves among;
Their curling heads are flashing bright
In the high noon's golden light
  As they dance and roll along :
Anon Jarl Rollo's trumpet-call
Burst from his towering castle-wall;
From cliff to cliff the echoes ring,
First shrill and then diminishing,
Until they mingle with the roar
Of the wild waves bounding on the shore;
Or die away upon the breeze
Marching stiffly over the seas.

V.

The Norsemen gathered round their chief,
Of thousands four, whose words were brief,
　　But sturdy men to do:
They would make their own their leader's grief,
　　And follow him Ocean through.
" Good friends," said he, " Our Danish King
　　Hath little work for those
Who love to hear the sea-winds sing,
　　And the battle shout of foes:
T'were little use to loiter here
　　Whilst in the South there are
Fair realms, of which with sword and spear
　　We may win a goodly share.
My flag you see waves from yon' mast;
　　It chideth all delay ;
The winds and tides are rising fast
　　To hurry us away:
So, let the burly North winds come,
　　And drive us where they please,
For our good blades must win a home
　　Ere we can sit at ease."

VI.

Then once more pealed the trumpet's bray
   From the rocks unto the shores;
Galley and bark shot from the bay,
Amidst the glistening showers of spray
   Raised by a thousand oars
To their war-songs beating the time,
Whilst their harness clashed in chime;
And they bounded o'er the foaming deep
As a steed will plunge and leap
When he hears the deer-hounds' bay,
And the hunters call away.

VII.

Jarl Rollo from his galley's prow
   Far strained his eagle eye;
The winds were breathing soft and slow;
   Bright stars were in the sky;
Over the tiny waves beneath
   The moonbeams shed their light,
Weaving many a silver wreath

For ocean elf and sprite,
To deck their pigmy forms withal
    When they come forth at night
To dance and keep high festival,
    Or hold some mystic rite.
The ancient Scald, who leaneth there
    On the harp he loves so well,
With his white locks on his head all bare
Streaming upon the midnight air,
    His master's thoughts can tell:
He sang to him, when boyhood dreamed,
    Tales of his warrior sires;
He sang to him, when victory gleamed,
And the banner of his father streamed
    O'er slaughtered foemen's pyres.
The old man knew his chieftain's mood;
    So, when the breezes slept
And hushed the murmurs of the flood,
    The strings of his harp he swept
To those tales and songs he loved of yore
    Anent the Norsemen old,
Of Odin too, and mighty Thor,

And of each famous ancestor,
   From whom his life-blood roll'd.

VIII.

But Rollo, with a spell-bound look,
   Still gazed upon the sky,
There was a stifled sigh which shook
   The pearl-drop in his eye;
For we may not say it was a tear,
   It would chafe his heart, I know;
His deep voice faltered, not with fear,
   As he spoke, but in accents low:
" My fatherland, and those old rocks
   I see before me still,
Or is it phantasy now mocks
   These eyes which seek to fill
The vacant chambers of my heart,
   With stores whereon may feed
Lone memory, in that distant part
   To which our vessels speed.

Thy shores may seem all dark and stern,
　　But they are the nursing place
Of bold Sea-Kings, whose roving turn
　　Plants many a gallant race
In fairer countries, and although
　　We sever in ill mood,
A recreant son were he I trow,
　　Who, in such evil blood,
Could say his last farewell to thee,
　　And take his parting look,
The last that it shall ever be,
And shut thee from his memory,
All light of heart and recklessly,
　　As idle child his book.
Another glance—aye, one more glance,
　　And the struggle within is done,
For the brisk waves on which we dance,
　　Await the morning sun ;
And I must rouse my slumbering men
　　To greet him with a song,
'Till the arched heavens send back again
　　Their voices deep and strong."

IX.

Then up from sleep each Norseman sprang,
    Already dressed in mail; *
Their voices in loud chorus rang
    As they bade their Chief all hail:
And whilst they sailed, the fearless crew
    Would laugh when the billows raved;
Or, if the winds more roughly blew,
They talk'd of the storms they had passed through,
    And the perils they had braved.
And, thus along the rolling sea,
The Danish boats sped gallantly;
Each mounting over every wave,
    And down into its trough;
Then rising like a warrior brave,
    Who hath dashed his foeman off.
The wild sea-horses raced in fun
    Around them and behind;
Their white manes glistened in the sun,
    And floated away on the wind.

From his unfathomable bed,
Old Ocean raised his elfin head
  The rioters to see,
Who dared on his domains to tread;
  And full of wrath was he;
From North to South, from West to East,
  He tossed himself about;
But I wot it mattered not the least
Whether his rage waxed more, or ceased,
  For still with song and shout,
They coursed along the hills of foam,
  Watching with careless eyes,
The porpoise rolling in his home,
  And the sea-birds in the skies.

X.

And now they held debate awhile,
  Where they should bend their way;
They had heard of a pleasant isle
  Which somewhere Southward lay:

There were some who knew the land of yore,
  And they said, that without much toil
They could land their troops upon the shore,
As often they had done before,
  And had won a goodly spoil.
So, forthwith to the South they steered
  Before a kindly breeze;
Long and lustily they cheered,
When the first line of cliffs appeared,
  Streaking the dark green seas;
Old England's these, a fairer sight
  Eye never looks upon,
When full upon each rock and bight
  Gleameth the morning sun;
When the blue waters roll along
  Under a light breeze crisping,
Whilst the waves raise a tiny song,
  Like that of an infant lisping;
But now, along the winding sands,
  And the far inland hills,
The sunbeams flash on bright steel brands,
  Spear-heads and bonny bills.

King Alfred, he the good and wise,
   And stout of heart withal,
Had said, " They shall not find a prize
   Easy to win at all."
Those stalwart Earls who round him stood
   Watching the stranger fleet,
Every one was in the same mood,
For the sight of the Raven chafed their blood
   Till it was in fever heat.

XI.

But whilst the fleet was bearing on
   Full steadily and fast
Towards the English shores, anon
   The clarion's startling blast
Echoed along the murmuring seas;
   The stately sea-mew spread
Her snowy pinions on the breeze,
   And whistled as she fled:
The signal passed throughout the fleet,
   Changed every bark her course;

Their Captain hath not deemed it meet
    To waste his gallant force .
Against a nation in its might
    In battle order found,
Prest to contest in steady fight,
    Aye, every inch of ground;
To spill in such unequal strife
    His faithful Norsemen's blood,
He thought a sinful waste of life,
    And wanton hardihood:
Discretion, it is somewhere writ,
    Is valour's better part;
And I'm sure the sequel proveth it
    However stout the heart.

XII.

A cloud came over Rollo's brow,
    And ill at ease he felt,
It liked him not to quit a foe
So gallant, and not strike a blow,
    Whilst his sword slept in his belt.

Thought he, " Yon' Islanders of late
   More stout of heart have grown ;
Their King held up a mace of weight,
And sat his battle steed-elate,
   As Woden on his throne.
I marked the Saxons as they stood
   In battle line so firm,
Like the oak trees in their native wood,
   And I wot as sound in germ—
We'll try the shores of merry France
   Which lie beyond these waters;
There are lands to win by sword and lance,
For the men are given to dalliance,
And Charles, their king, may like, perchance,
   To mate us with his daughters.
Carry us faster then, kind gales ;
   Blow lustily, if ye will;
We can sing our songs and tell our tales,
   And stride the sea-horses still.

XIII.

Night crept along the heavens; the wind
   Sunk moaningly to sleep;
Then a magic silence seemed to bind
   The waters of the deep;
The lady Moon sailed forth to see
   How she had charmed old Ocean,
Who bowed beneath her reverently
   Like a monk at his devotion.
At length Jarl Rollo felt the spell
   Over his senses creeping;
A mystic slumber on him fell,
How long he slept he could not tell,
   For still his eyes seemed keeping
Their anxious watch o'er sea and heaven,
   Whilst strange sights rose before him,
And forms not made of earthly leaven
   Hovered around and o'er him.
Anon uprose the ancient Thor,
   And thus he spoke to Rollo:

" Hail to thee, favored son of war;
   Success thy course shall follow;
A race of kings will spring from thee
Whose people shall be bold and free,
   And noble in their hearts;
Their fleets unconquered on the sea;
Their armies carrying victory
   To earth's remotest parts."
Thereat Jarl Rollo rose amain,
   Well pleased to think upon
The visions floating o'er his brain,
And bade his clarions sound again
   To greet the rising sun.

XIV.

Ere long, the smiling shores of France
   Rose looming from the sea;
Once more each Norseman shook his lance,
   And shouted lustily.
Soon as their galleys touched the strand,
Jarl Rollo drew his flashing brand,
   And waved it o'er his casque:

" Now we have set our feet on land,
   'Twill be no easy task
To drive us on the seas agen,
Come Charles with all his fighting men!
Hark ! there's a distant trumpet strain,
   I can hear armour clashing,
And the tramp of horse on yonder plain;—
   I see the spear-heads flashing
In the broad beams of Heaven's sun,
   And horsemen forward dashing ;
We shall have shortly warrior's fun,
   For the grove of silken banners floating,
Are march of mail-clad troops denoting :—
   Stand fast and firmly every one."

XV.

Of paladins in glittering steel,
   Two thousand twice came on ;
Each with golden spurs on heel,
   And a golden morion
Upon his head ; each had a steed

Mettled and hot, and choice in breed
As ever a good knight might need
  To shew menage upon;
Each one he had two squires who bore
  Shield, lance, and polish'd greaves;
And men-at-arms to each one four,
  Sturdy as working beeves.
In front rode Charles, his eye and cheek
  Shew'd nightly thought and care;
Full well he knew his force too weak
  To wage a battle there.
Next him on palfrey white as milk,
With bit of gold, and rein of silk,
  His daughter Gisla came:
Tho' sharing in her sire's distress,
All peerless she in loveliness;
  Throughout all France, her fame;
In simple vestments white as snow,
  One coronet of gold
Around her fair and noble brow
  Those flaxen ringlets hold.

Many a knight had broken lance,
  And goodly charger shent
To win from her eyes one kindly glance
  In the lists of tournament.

XVI.

The Northern Chief beheld the maid;
  He closed his barret cap:
" Those eyes are sharper than my blade;
I never felt so much afraid;
  I'll guard against mishap. "
Then, as he ranged his warrior band
In battle order on the strand,
  There was daring in each eye;
They brandished sword and rattled shield,
For they were in haste to win a field,
  And sure of a victory.

XVII.

King Charles who was a fearful wight,
　Though he was cased in steel,
Had little relish for a fight,
For in truth he could not tell the knight
Of all who stood in harness bright
　Whom he could trust as leal.
Said he to Rollo, " Prithee now
Good Chieftain, tell me, wherefore thou
　Hath landed on our plain,
With lance in hand and helm on brow
　And all this martial train ?"
Then answered Rollo: " I am he
　Far-famed throughout the North;
They call me Rollo the bold and free,
　And terrible in my wrath.
One evening when the tempest made
　Such stir among the billows,
That our Sea-Kings, not oft afraid,
　Cared not to leave their pillows,

There was a feast in Harfold's Hall,
And I the readiest of them all
The perils of the sea to dare,
Or council of the state to share;
I proferred suit, which he denied;
In sudden anger I defied
The thankless churl unto the death,
Our jarls astonished held their breath.
Straight I was banished, and these bands
Who had small love for Northern lands,
Followed my banner where the wind
Should waft our barks to realms more kind.
So here we doughty rovers are,
   And a home it is we seek;
This country seemeth free and fair;
   We have anchored in yon' creek:
We are all you see in fighting trim,
Stout in heart, and strong in limb,
   And ready for battle eke;
I swear by my father's sword and helm,
   As friends to thee or foe,
We'll take a part of this goodly realm,
   Whether you will or no."

XVIII.

Charles looked upon that sturdy host,
   And then on his mail-clad lords;
Thought he, my men, though given to boast,
Whenever danger is pressing most,
They are slack to use their swords:
" Brave Chieftain," I have land to spare,
   Which I will give to thee,
If thou on our Gospel Book wilt swear
As a good knight thyself to bear
To ourself and every future heir,
   And render fealty;
And Rollo, if thou art inclined
   A blushing maid to woo,
My daughter's hand shall more firmly bind
   The compact between us too.

XIX.

The Chieftain gazed upon the maid,
   And the sunny vales before him;
Strange feelings on his bold heart preyed,
I do not say he was afraid,

But a nervousness crept o'er him;
Behind him lay the slumbering sea,
Smooth as a polished glass was he,
  Which of late so roughly bore him;
So clear the crystal waters shone,
  You might see the depths below,
Where the sea-flowers on rock and stone
  In rich profusion grow:
Now ocean when he lieth at rest,
  Is a beauteous sight I ween,
It would soften the most rugged breast
  To look on so fair a scene;
There was not a cloud in the skies above,
  But a hallowed calm o'er all;
In sooth, 'twas more an hour for love
  Than for battle or for brawl.

XX.

Said Rollo, " By my good sword's hilt,
  The bargain liketh me,
So, fairest maiden, if thou wilt,
  I will wed with hearty glee."

Stepped forth the first Lord Seneschal,
   And thus spoke to the Chief;
" First on thy knees thou need'st must fall,
And in the presence of us all,
   Do homage for thy fief."
Ill words were these, for Rollo's ire
   Waxed hot as they were spoken;
He grasped his sword, his eyes flash'd fire—
" Now by the valour of my sire
   I fear this truce is broken.
It ne'er was seen and ne'er shall be,
That Rollo on his bended knee
   Bowed down to any man,
And certes such indignity
   Would anger all my clan."
The maiden's cheeks were blanched with fright
As each prepared him for the fight,
For they thought it must soon begin:
But Rollo held her hand within
His own, and in such tender mood
Pressing it as fond lover should,

Whispered something, that her eye
Soon recovered its brilliancy:
" I cannot list to have it said
    That Rollo broke a vow ;
My herald Sweyn shall bare his head,
And if it please thee, in my stead
    He shall do homage now."

XXI.

The stiff old Norseman strided out
Most unwillingly no doubt,
Scowling beneath his shaggy brows,
Rather would he have gone to blows,
But he knew his Chief would have his way,
'Twas not for him to say him nay;
King Charles sat on his royal chair
With his lords and mitred prelates there
Standing around, and overhead
The sacred banner of France outspread
Her folds that were magnificent
With the crimson and gold so richly blent.

The Dane stood there erect and tall
Frowning fiercely upon them all,
But when they said, " Thou must kneel down
To kiss his toe who wears the crown;"
(Such was the plan in days of yore,
   At least they tell us so,
Who are well versed in ancient lore,
   And I no better know);
He bore him most irreverently,
Vowing he would not bend his knee,
And he would kiss it as he stood;
Then he seized the foot in such rough mood,
That he rolled the unsuspecting king
From his throne, amidst the courtly ring,
   And sprawling on the floor he lay;
Whether this were a wilful thing,
   Or accident, I cannot say.

XXII.

Charles looked around upon his lords;
They frowned indeed, and grasped their swords,

And they uttered curses deep,
But their rage found vent in idle words,
  And soon it fell asleep.
Each Norseman laughed right heartily
  To see the King's mischance;
Fair Gisla's eyes looked pleadingly,
Bold Rollo felt their witchery
  And quailed beneath her glance :
" 'Tis time to quaff a health," said he,
  " To this fair maid of France:
Bring me the mighty wassail cup,
  That graced my father's hall,
To healths and pledges fill it up
  Until the night-clouds fall.
Charles saw 'twas idle to resent,
  Nor would his anger last:
" I think time would be better spent
If one and all within our tent,
  Would share in our repast."
The Knights of France were true and leal,
  Not one would thwart King Charles ;
Rollo threw down his cap of steel
  And answered for his Jarls:

Their armour doffed these Northern men,
  And sheathed their idle brands,
The French knights came around, and then
  They one and all shook hands.
The feast was held till eventide,
  And all went merrily,
Without a brawl to fright the bride
Who graced the seat by Rollo's side,
  Tho' strange it seems to be.

XXIII.

Then when the holy priest came near
  Of Gospel truths to tell,
Rollo turned not away his ear,
  And Gisla's tears fast fell,
To see how that bold Chief did list
  To the mysterious Word,
Dispelling every heathen mist
  As each new truth was heard;
Yes, she wept joyfully and long,
  And thankfully she prayed,
When in the church they raised a song
  As his Christian pledge he made;

And they signed the Holy Cross upon
  His brow so high and bold;
He stepped from the church a heathen won
  From the evil spirit's hold.

XXIV.

Thus Rollo gained a lovely wife
  With rich and goodly lands,
And he passed the remnant of his life
In making laws to hinder strife
  And govern his warrior bands.
They called his realm fair Normandy,
  And him a Duke they name;
It was one of his posterity
  Who our England's King became;
For Norman William, he who won
  The crown from Harold's brow,
Was Rollo's grandson's great grandson:
  The Queen who rules us now,

Traces her life-blood to that fount
  In straight ascending line;
Long may she live that throne to mount
  Her's by a right divine :
And after her, her issue true,
  Long may they hold the Crown
Against the democratic crew,
  Who would seek to hurl it down.

The Death of Edward the Martyr.

A.D. 978.

It is almost unnecessary to say here that the whole of this tale, except the murder of the King by one of his stepmother's servants whilst drinking on horseback before the gate of Corfe Castle, where she resided, is fiction. It would be difficult to account for his being called the Martyr, but the extracts from Hume which I have subjoined will relieve me from the charge of having done so without authority, and will throw a little light upon the character of the Prince.

"This young Prince was endowed with the most amiable innocence of manners, and as his own intentions were pure, he was incapable of entertaining any suspicion against others. Though his stepmother (Elfrida) had opposed his succession, and had raised a party in favour of her own son, he always shewed her marks of regard, and even expressed on all occasions the most tender affection towards his brother."

*   *   *

"The youth and innocence of the Prince, with his tragical death, begat such compassion among the people, that they believed miracles to be wrought at his tomb, and they gave him the appellation of Martyr, though his murder had no connection with any religious principle or opinion." —HUME.

The Death of Edward the Martyr.

LADY ELLA resteth long
  On her bridal bed;
If her sleep be sweet as strong,
  Break it not by noisy tread.
It was a lovely sight to see
The features' perfect tracery;
Over her brow and dimpled cheek
Blushing rose and lily seek
How to blend in harmony;
Through her lips half-opened peer
Teeth than richest pearl more clear,
And upon her snowy breast
Silken ringlets clustering rest.

II.

But anon she starts and weeps,
   And her light frame seems to shake,
As when a soft zephyr sweeps
   Over a placid lake.
By that smothered shriek and wild
Like the cry of frightened child,
   She is sadly dreaming;
Ave Maria! Virgin mild!
Chase away the evil power,
Guard her until morning hour,
   And the sun is gleaming.

III.

Ella suddenly upstarted,
And by the wild looks she darted
On her maidens each and all,
Rushing to her hasty call,
You had thought her reason flown
Far away from its own throne;

But as the young sunlight fell
Glancing through the oriel,
And the odours of sweet flowers
Wafted from the garden bowers,
Mingling with the May-morn air,
Breathed their fragrant essence there,
Whilst the skylark's carroling
Made the span of Heaven ring,
Soon all phantom terrors fled,
And in her soft eyes were shed
Smiles of youthful joyousness,
Bright from her pure heart's recess.

IV.

Then Ella turned her azure eye
Around her chamber eagerly,
Her Saxon maidens tend her now
To smooth the tresses on her brow;
She whispered into Brenda's ear,
" I've been a lazy one I fear,
Or else some weighty matters stir
My Edward to rise earlier."

Said Brenda, " If I guess not wrong
  This is a hunting-day,
The blast of the horn was loud and strong,
The foresters trilled forth a song
  Soon as the morning grey
Had thrown her russet streaks along
  The heaven's Eastern bay,
And it was told us but last night,
By Ceobald, a shepherd wight,
That every evening after dark,
The dog-wolf hath been heard to bark ;
  Our shepherds dare not sleep
Until the rising of the lark,
  But midnight watch must keep
Beside their folds ; our castle maids
  After the vesper chimes,
Roam not amongst the forest glades,
  But hasten home betimes :
I therefore guess our royal King
Hath summoned here a gathering
  Of lords and yeomanry :
They reckon on a good day's chase,
To find the stranger's lurking place;

For since the last decree
King Edgar made, the land to clear
  From horrid beasts of prey,
Three hundred wolf-heads every year
  Our neighbouring Welsh should pay.
The brutes grow scarce, and scarcer still
They should be, if I had my will,
  For our old wives do say,
Lambs are not their only food,
Woman and child they reckon as good
  When they come in their way."

v.

Much more the prattling maid had said,
Nor marked the ashy change which spread
  Over her lady's cheek ;
The tidings she hath told perchance
Reminds her of her midnight trance,
  Though she may fear to speak,
And strives to brush her tears away
Lest they should laugh at her dismay.

Yet must she see her loving mate
Before he leaves the castle-gate ;
Each one she so hurrieth
They can scarcely take their breath ;
From her robing room she flies
   Like a child unto it's sport,
Through the banquet-hall she hies
   Unto the outer court:
The morning air was stiff and keen,
For this she little cared, I ween,
Yet it will her maids displease
When they see the morning breeze
All those silken ringlets spoil
Which have cost them care and toil.

VI.

And now upon the dewlit sward,
   The royal hounds were sporting,
Boar spear flashed, and hunting sword,
   And mettled steeds were snorting.

The master ranger blew a note
  Upon his silver horn,
Far away its echoes float
  To the distant forest bourn;
Then upon the castle-wall
Faint and dyingly they fall.
Passed the ale cup merrily,
  Stout healths some were drinking;
A solemn fool they thought was he
  Who sat still a-thinking.
And as the good cheer they quaffed,
Many an old spearman laughed
To hear the idle younkers prate,
  As they rode to and fro,
And tongues run on in boastful rate,
  Of what they meant to do.

VII.

A gallant courser standing yare,
  Yon' page can scarcely hold,
He snuffs his fill of the fresh air
  And champeth his bit of gold;

Upon his back the King will sit,
Surely the good steed knoweth it,
By his proud and fiery eye,
And his head held up on high,
Tossing the white froth around
As he stands and paws the ground.
There stood Edward, gay in mien,
Clad in suit of forest green,
A noble King to look upon,
Though but an unbearded one,
For not yet the youth had seen
Eighteen rounds of summer's sun,
But his lieges loved him well,
As saith ancient chronicle,
And his bride was England's boast
From the North hills to Southern coast;
Ever on village green or throne
Lovelier maiden was not known;
But ill dreams had driven away
The rose that on her cheek should play,
And the bright smile in her eye
Seemed to vanish away and die.

VIII.

Said Edward to his trembling bride,
As he brushed her locks aside,
" Why hath Ella left her bed?
   Why is her cheek so pale?
Those witching eyes seem moist and red
As though some tear-drops had been shed;
   Love, let me hear thy tale.
Is there aught I have forgot?
Thinketh she I love her not?"
Said Ella " If thou lovest me
And I were ever dear to thee,
   I pray thee do not go.
See how thy banner on yon' tower
   Droopeth its folds so low,
Every field and garden flower
Hangeth her head as when storms lour;
   And evil forms of woe
Haunted me in my hours of sleep
Last night: Oh! leave me not to weep
   Lay down thy spear and bow;

Young Edgar will supply thy place,
And Dorset's Earl can lead the chase;
   Thou heed'st not what I say.
Edgar, I pray thee lend a word!"
" Nay, Lady, if thou art not heard,
I cannot hope to be preferred :
   The King will have his way."

IX.

Young Edward gazed upon his bride;
   He loved her heartily;
Ill could he brook the pearly tide
   Fast chasing from her eye;
Full loth was he to say her nay,
And still more loth behind to stay,
For the sun in his bright chariot
   Was sailing gloriously
Through the arched heavens, where no spot
   Nor vapour could you see,
Whilst the merry hunters' strains
Echoed along the castle plains,

Where eager hounds were baying
And prancing coursers neighing.
When the heart's wish once is set
   Who likes to have it broken?
I would make a trifling bet
Ella's self would not be let
   To do what she had spoken.

X.

Edward whispered in her ear,
  (What loving words he said
None were near enough to hear,)
But it did not soothe her fear,
  For she gently bowed her head,
Though she smiled, to hide a tear,
That smile had but a sickly gleam,
  And it spoke of coming sorrow,
Like the gleam of the sun in heaven's stream
For it ever is a sign I deem
  Of rain upon the morrow.
" Thou flower of Saxon daughters,
Ere the moonbeams touch the waters

I will set me by thy side,
　And will kiss thy tears away,
Whilst we watch the sparkling tide
　Dashing on in its wild play."
He hath kissed her once and twice
　On her lip and cheek and brow ;
He hath vaulted in a trice
　On his gallant courser now ;
They have galloped o'er the plain,
　And have reached the furthest hills ;
They are rushing down again ;
　They have leaped across the rills;
And now are lost within the shades
Of the wide forest's darksome glades.

XI.

But faster rose Queen Ella's fears,
And faster chased the crystal tears
　Adown her pallid cheek ;
Still fancy many a vision rears
　Too horrible to speak;

She strained her eye to catch the last
And loving glance her Edward cast;
And as the echoes died away
Of horses' tramp, and wolf-hounds' bay,
The lady sought her garden bower,
   And bade her maidens sing
To wile away the heavy hour;
And then she plucked a summer flower:
Alas! that none of these had power
   To check her sorrowing:
For when the heart is ill at ease,
There's nothing eye or ear can please;
   Around us every thing
Will bring remembrance of our grief;
E'en mirth, if it give respite brief,
   A darker shade will fling,
When the wild thought hath sobered down
Under the pangs it seemed to drown,
   Perchance, a deeper sting.
And now before St. Wilfred's shrine
   Ella all humbly kneeleth;
On earth she bends her tearful eyne,

Offering prayers for aid divine,
And oft she makes the holy sign
   Whilst the solemn music peeleth:
Priests are in the sacred pile;
Beads they tell, and prayers the while;
Their mingling voices deep and clear
   Poured forth from that long train,
Now rise, now sink upon the ear,
   In penitential strain.

*   *   *   *

XII.

The cricket raised her even-song
The bracken glades and banks among;
And the night-owl sweepeth by,
Peering with his twinkling eye
Where the silken field mouse playeth,
Or some luckless birdling strayeth;
The lazy bat is on his wing,
From his dark hole wandering:
The bells in yonder abbey tower
Are tolling for the vesper hour:

If you listen you will hear
Chaunt of priests steal on the ear;
Let them raise your heart within
Thoughts above this world of sin;
'Tis a changeful one at best,
Even unto those who rest
Under the sheen of fortune's smiles,
Or may bask in pleasure's wiles.
The Sun was on his nether march
In the heaven's Western arch,
Flooding with his purple light
Mountain top and ocean bight;
Standing as it were between
Yourself and that all glorious sheen,
Corfe Castle's walls and turrets grey
Rose darkling o'er the lone highway;
A horse-foot rings upon the ground,
Its echoes on the walls resound;
The warder on his watch intent,
Looked down from the battlement
   Upon the pass below;
Then loudly he began to call
Within to the old seneschal:

" There's England's King beneath the wall,
  Let Queen Elfrida know ;
For doubtless she will deem it right
To give him welcome for the night."
When Edward found that he was seen,
  But little pleased was he ;
For ever since he had left his Queen,
Ill at ease his heart had been,
  And he rode all moodily
The cheerful foresters among,
Heeding neither jest nor song,
  Nor sharing in their glee.
" I may not pass my mother's gate,
  Nor ask how fares her grace ;
For though she bears me in her hate,
'Tis best to shew at any rate,
  I do not shun her face."

XIII.

Then went the ancient seneschal
Unto his lady in her hall,
  Bowing him reverently,
As should a duteous menial ;

Till bidden, spoke not he.
" What tidings doth old Hubert bring
That he leaves watch and guard?"
Answereth he: " Our England's King
Is coming hitherward;
Returning homeward from the chase,
He tenders duty to your grace,
And asks a benizon
For him and for his lady bride."
" What train attends our son?
What lords and vassals with him ride?
Is the fair Ella at his side?
Or cometh he alone?"
Said he: " Our lord seems tired and sad;
Blown and weary seems his pad;
Of lords and vassals, none
Are with him now; he left his train
To seek his lady's bowers again,
Where many hours agone
He quitted her in tearful vein."
A furtive glance of glad surprise
Sparkled in Elfrida's eyes:

" Hie thee, good Hubert, to the gate;
Tarry the King by idle prate,
Whilst I don kirtle, hood, and veil
To shield my face from evening gale;
And the wassail bowl my maid shall take,
If his thirst he wish to slake—
There is a business to be done
Must not be told to every one."
The seneschal with lowly bow
Leaveth the Lady's presence now :
And she calleth her little page,
Nimble in foot, though young in age:
" Hie thee now, thou elvish midge,
Like an arrow, to the bridge
Beside the tall hill, where the brook
Eddies in its unfathomed nook;
None that plunged in that dark wave
Ever were laid in earthen grave :
Wend to the right along the bank
Where the rushes grow tall and dank ;
Fifty paces, and fifty more
Will bring you to a mean hut's door :

Cough three times, and give knocks three,
A black brow'd man will come to thee;
Speak him not, but give this ring,
Then hasten back with an eagle's wing:
When my bidding thou hast done
See thou speak of it to none."

XIV.

The young page scoured o'er hill and dale;
He reached the bottom of the vale;
He turned the bridge just where the brook
Eddied and curled in its dark nook:
The waters there were sullen and deep;
And the banks were high and steep;
The gaunt old trees, withered and dead,
Stretched their scath'd arms overhead;
They looked like giant skeletons,
The soughing wind might be their moans:
Shuddered the page from limb to limb
As the eft and toad crept under him.
The moon was hid under a cloud,
It seemed to him like dead man's shroud.

Said he, " I have heard of this lone man,

Dreaded and shunned by all our clan;

Murdock they give him for a name;

No one knoweth whence he came ;

'Tis said his face he dare not lift

To the high heavens, and no shrift

Priest will ever give to him,

When his eyes in death grow dim;

Youth like me might fear to come

Nigh to such a lonesome home;

Demon or mortal he may be

If my lady pay me handsomely." .

Fifty paces and fifty more,

And he stood the lowly hut before :

He coughed three times and he knocked thrice,

His blood within him seemed turning ice;

Slowly it opened and there stands,

He who will do the Queen's commands :

His long lank hair fell on his breast,

And his dark eyes never seemed to rest,

But they met not the light, nor open glance,

They looked down, or else askance :

" Springald, what dost thou want with me,
  Do thy message speedily."
So the page took out his lady's ring,
And gave to the strange man, shuddering.

XV.

Meanwhile sat Edward on his steed,
    Without the castle gate;
Old Hubert praised the courser's breed,
His tongue ran on in idle speed,
    And with an old man's prate:
He said there was a time when he
Was skilled in sports of venery;
Stout as any he could ride
Over hill, or stem a tide;
But the grey locks on his head
Told that his best hours were fled;
Soon the church bells' muffled tones
Would toll whilst they laid his old bones
Deep within his mother earth;
Till then he had a goodly berth:

" But my old tongue runs babbling on ;
My Lady will be here anon
With some goodly fare for thee,
Which she offers lovingly ;
And the wine which she will bring,
Meet it is for Earl or King.

XVI.

The castle gate was opened wide,
Elfrida came in stately pride,
[1] Lawless Edgar's widowed Queen,
Haughtier woman ne'er was seen;
And her eyes were still as bright
    As when Earl Athelwold
First beheld their witching light
That lured him from the course of right,
    Which duteous vassals hold
To their liege lords, and he betrayed
The trust which in his faith was laid ;
Aye, still upon her cheek and brow
The rose and lily even now

Mingled their rich and native hue
As though Time owned the homage due
  Unto her peerless beauty,
And feared in his deep reverence
To pluck a single charm from thence,
  So well he kept his duty;
A fair young maid behind her walked
Who ne'er with glance of eye had talked;
Golden cup and flask she bore,
Filled I trow with luscious store;
Sweetmeats made by her fair hands
Holds the youth who next her stands:
There were serving men and maids
  Eke in the lady's train,
Vassals from the forest glades
Bearing spears and glittering blades,
  Who called her Sovereign;
Doing her bidding day and night,
Nor nice to question what was right.

XVII.

Young Edward took but little heed
　Of any who stood there,
Or else I think he had seen need
To watch them well, or make good speed,
Such felon's looks some wore indeed,
　And darker looks are rare:
But thoughts of evil, or that lacked
Of charity, had not yet tracked
　Their course to his young heart:
If he then had scanned them well,
There would have been no tale to tell
　To point the poet's art.
Seldom it is when life is young,
　And youthful hopes are beating high,
And ere the heart hath been among
　The schools of treachery,
We dream of falsehood or deceit;
　Such tales are whispered in the ear
And fables deemed: those whom we meet
　We have no cause to fear:

Fair words and sweet are spoken, smiles
    Wreath sunnily upon each brow,
Who dares to breathe that they are guiles
    To mark a secret foe !
Suspicion ! check the inkling glance
    Unworthy youth's free heart and mien,
Not yet on that fresh countenance
    The traces can be seen
Of plighted truth to falsehood dyed ;
    Affection's blossoms one by one
Found scentless, or perchance to hide
    The thorn that racks our own.
Alas ! that ever promises
    So bright should all so quickly perish ;
Yet who shall say my picture is
    Too darkly drawn for all we cherish.

XVIII.

Gallantly Edward bowed his head,
And his brows unbonneted
    To greet his fair step-mother ;

He questioned her of health and weal,
(For he had little to conceal,)
 And of his younger brother.
With silvery voice and witching eye
Answered the lady lovingly:
" Now may our Holy Mother's blessing
 Rest on our England's King;
In yon' church I've been confessing
 The deeds of my life's spring.
I pray thee pardon my delay,
 But when concerns of heaven are pressing
All earthly forms give way.
But why art thou so late, my son?
 For night draws on apace,
And traitors through our realms do run
 With shameless front and face.
I will not stay thee from thy bride,
For she hath wept since morning tide;
Yet I may ask thee to partake
 A cup of goodly mead:
The dust from off thy mantle shake,
 Then Heaven give thee good speed."

XIX.

Edward took the golden cup:
  " A health to all," said he;
Then to his lips he left it up
  And drank right heartily.
I wot he had been thirsting long,
The draught he took was deep and strong.
Dark Murdock's eyes his Lady's sought,
And glances, with full meaning fraught,
  Between the two were given;
" At last young Edward thou art caught—
  What lucky chance hath driven
Our bird so soon to the snare we've wrought—
  Pray that his sins be shriven."
Heaven warn the young and innocent,
Or foil the murderer's intent !
All cautiously the felon stole
Behind the King as he drained the bowl:
Anon, there was a sudden start;
A shriek that pierced the very heart;

The whole frame shuddered and turned cold
As forth the warm red life-stream roll'd,
And as it spread along the ground
   'Twas a contrast sickening
To the dew drops which lay around
   In the moonlight glittering.
But Edward, finding he did not fall,
   Cried out, as he spurr'd his steed,
" Madam, no thanks to you at all;
   Thou hast not done the deed :
And if I reach my castle-hall,
To-morrow our royal seneschal
Our Thanes to the judgment-seat shall call,
   And pay thee as thou dost meed."
Then forward on the wings of the wind
   Rider and courser started;
In the morning the traveller will find
The tracks where the blood-stream fell behind,
   Until the soul departed.

*   *   *

XX.

Already it was the midnight hour;
Ella is watching in her bower;
She hath sat there the livelong day,
Wiling the lonely hours away. .
'Twas such a night the young do love
   When their light hearts may soar
On the free wings of thought above,
   Or by the magic shore
Of fancy's strange imaginings,
   When shadows of the past
From her far regions memory brings
   In changing crowds and fast,
Showing the soul's delighted eye,
A sweet and cherished tracery,
   Then cheating them at last.
There was a soughing of the breeze
Amidst the sombre forest trees ;
The solitary nightingale
Trilled her melancholy tale ;
And ever as the night-wind sighed,
It was echoed on the tide,

Whose waters doled a mournful lay
As they danced and rolled away;
And to the artificial throng,
Their wild notes as they swept along,
Might have no touch of harmony;
But I deem there is rich minstrelsy
In gurgling rills or rushing streams
  And ocean's deeper roar,
That singeth to the heart of themes
  She loveth evermore.

XXI.

There is a sound in Ella's ears
  Ever ringing mournfully;
Was it a voice from yonder spheres,
Far beyond this vale of change and tears,
Where the bright spirits of the blest
Are hymning in their eternal rest
  To the glorious Trinity?
It cometh again, and seems to her
Like the summons of death's minister.

Her brain seemed fire, her heart was chill,
She kept her eye on the heavens still;
There was a little pause in the sound,
A dark form moved along the ground;
(A shriek that startled every bird
And deer, from his bracken lair was heard;)
Nigher it came, trying to speak,
The sound was lost, for the tongue was weak;
It fell, and the rattle in the throat
Was the last sound the ear could note :
" Merciful Heaven! I see thee now;
The chestnut locks on thy high brow
Are matted with dust and ruby gore;
Thou hast a wound, 'tis not before;
Thou hast not fallen in the chase,
 Nor met an enemy
As thou wouldst meet him, face to face
 And sword to sword, but treachery
Hath done its evil work on thee."

   *   *   *

XXII.

The castle maidens were asleep,
Their slumbers had been long and deep;
It was not till the morning sun
One quarter of his course had run,
When Emmeleen whose was the care
That morn to deck her lady's hair,
Wondering no summons had been heard,
Waked Brenda, who had not yet stirred,
　To take an early walk;
Brenda was merry as a bird
　And lively in her talk,
And saith she to Emmeleen,
" Where hath our royal master been?
Never should husband of my own,
E'en tho' he sat on England's throne,
Tarry from me a single night
Keeping me the while in fright;
　Our lady could not rest:
I watched her in the pale moonlight,
　Roaming like one distressed;

I shall marvel, if ere night come round,

We hear not tidings of ill sound;

For surely one who seemed to love

So dearly never could faithless prove."

Then sauntering through bower and dell,

They talked of themes which maids love well:

The one praised wealth and power and rank;

The other deemed them all a blank:

She said love was a gift from heaven

Richer than ought of earthly leaven,

When troth for troth and heart for heart

 In very singleness were given,

And bonds such as death scarce can part

 In true affection riven.

Scarce had they reached the woodland bound,

When turning suddenly around,

Each frightened maiden gave a start—

" Holy St. Mary! who lies there!

 'Twas Ella, beautiful and fair;

By her Edward's corpse she lay,

But the lamp of life had flitted away.

   *   *   *

The thrush and the lark sang merrily
As their spirits soared on high,
From the fetters of dull earth set free
To the thrones beyond the sky.

(1) *" The lawless Edgar,"*—S. xvi. p. 58.

I have made use of this term in reference only to the means by which Edgar obtained the hand of Elfrida, and to other enormous offences against morality and religion which he committed. In other respects he appears to have been a wise and politic prince, not altogether incompetent or unwilling to frame laws for the benefit of his people.

The Escape of Prince Edward.

1265.

The following extracts from HUME will show the foundation of the following tale:

"Leicester, who possessed great talents for war, conducted his march with such skill and secresy, that he had well nigh surprised the royalists in their quarters at Lewes, in Sussex ; but the vigilance and activity of Prince Edward soon repaired this negligence, and he led out the king's army to the field in three bodies. * * * *

"May 14, Prince Edward rushed on the Londoners who had demanded the post of honour in leading the rebel army, but who, from their ignorance of discipline and want of experience, were ill fitted to resist the gentry and military men of whom the prince's body was composed; and Edward, transported by his martial ardour, and eager to revenge the insolence of the Londoners against his mother, put them to the sword for the length of four miles. * * * * The Earl of Leicester, seeing the royalists thrown into confusion by their eagerness in pursuit, led on his remaining troops against the bodies commanded by the two royal brothers (Henry III. and the King of the Romans): he defeated with great slaughter the forces headed by the King of the Romans, and that prince was obliged to yield himself prisoner to the Earl of Gloucester: he penetrated to the body where

E

the king was placed, threw it into disorder, pursued his advantage, chased it into the town of Lewes, and obliged Henry to surrender himself prisoner.

" Prince Edward, returning to the field of battle from his precipitate pursuit of the Londoners, was astonished to find it covered with the dead bodies of his friends. * * * * * He found his followers intimidated by their situation. * * * * * There now appeared no further resource to the royal party, surrounded by the army and garrison of the enemy; * * * the prince, therefore, was obliged to submit to Leicester's terms. The prince and young Henry accordingly delivered themselves into Leicester's hands.

*   *   *   *   *   *

" The Earl of Gloucester concerted with young Edward the manner of that prince's escape. He found means to convey to him a horse of extraordinary swiftness, and appointed Roger Mortimer to be ready at hand with a small party to receive the prince, and to guard him to a place of safety. Edward pretended to take the air with some of Leicester's retinue, who were his guards, (May 28th,) and making matches with their horses; after he thought he had tried and blown them sufficiently, he suddenly mounted Gloucester's horse, and called to his attendants that he had long enough enjoyed the pleasure of their company, and now bid them adieu. They followed him for sometime without being able to overtake him, and the appearance of Mortimer with his company put an end to their pursuit."

The Escape of Prince Edward.

NEAR Lewes met the rebel Earls—
   Old Montfort was their chief ;
And leagued with these were losel churls
  From many a baron's fief,
Whom a discontented spirit stirs ;
And eke the merry Londoners
Under old Segrave gathering,
Went forth to fight against their King.
A motley looking host were they
As ever in battle order lay :
Their scowling brows and downcast eyes
Spoke an unrighteous enterprise :

But there were some of knightly rank
  And barons of degree,
Who at first from treason's cup had drank,
  Now came unwillingly;
For skilled was Simon Montfort's tongue
  To lure and overreach;
He could make it seem that right was wrong,
  Such was his glozen speech.
There was Earl Gloucester, Gilbert Clare,
  And stout Earl Hereford.
Why do they bring their vassals there
  Against their own liege lord?
But what saith he of Chichester
  The mitred lord and priest?
Surely the holy messenger
  Will teach them right at least—
He giveth pardon full and free
  To each, and unto all,
And a seat in heaven eternally,
  Who in the fight shall fall:
Oh! Prelate, what saith Holy Writ?
  " Honour the King," you know,

And thinkest thou 'tis meet and fit
   To praise his rebel foe ?

II.

The royal troops shewed gallant head,
And these young Edward Longshanks led,
   King Henry's eldest son;
The Earls and Barons who were leal
With stout retainers sheathed in steel,
   In proud array came on;
There were Bruce, Warrenne, and Grosvenor,
   Hugh Bigod, and stout Blount,
Young Comyn from the Northern shore,
With many a doughty Baron more,
And than each no braver warrior
   On battle steed could mount;
Every face shone fair and bright
With the consciousness of right,
   And heartily they cheered,
When o'er their lines the youngest knight
   The royal standard reared.

III.

Awhile the fortunes of the day
In doubtful chances seemed to play ;
First on the rebels it would shine,
Then full upon the royal line ;
   The Londoners gave way
Before the charge of Edward's van,
With whom the conflict first began,
For full of wrath was he, I ween
   Those sturdy citizens to see,
Who had with language vile and mean
   And many a foul indignity,
Treated his mother, Henry's Queen.
Too quickly Edward gave the word
That every knight with lance and sword
Should chase the villains from the field ;
And these, too desperate to yield,
   Unsteadily retreated ;
Yet Leicester in another part,
Meanwhile with troops of better heart,
   Stood firm and undefeated ;

And as young Edward led the chase,
His men broke from their ranks apace ;
It was in faith a mighty flaw ;
The wary Earl his vantage saw,
  The battle in his grasp ;
He shouted long and lustily,
" Come, merry hearts and stand by me,
  They are at their last gasp."

IV.

Against the royal cause, once more
The changes of the fight went sore :
King Henry fought with feeble hand
Alone amidst the rebel band ;
The choicest of his knights were gone
In hot pursuit with his brave son ;
And sorely was he pressed indeed,
When underneath him fell his steed ;
Then Leicester charging up again
Took prisoner his liege Sovereign ;

Whilst with his early vantage flushed
Back to the strife young Edward rushed,
Sad was his wonderment to find
The field with victor rebels lined,
Where many a loyal Baron laid
Grasping in death his shivered blade.
The cause was lost, the scale had turned,
Earl Leicester hath the victory earned.
'Twas hopeless to prolong the fight
When every loyal Earl and Knight
Lay dying, or had left the field,
Or pledged his knightly word to yield;
So Edward sought for Gilbert Clare,
The Earl, thought he, seemed ever fair,
And is of honourable bent,
Though now he joins the rebels' tent,
No other Earl shall take my sword:
And in good time comes Gloucester's lord;
" Sir Gilbert, sithence Heaven this day
    Hath given thee victory,
Take thou my sword, and lead away,
    Nor care I were it be ;

I little dreamed to find thee here
  In arms against our right:
How sits thine honour? Is it clear?
  Art not a perjured Knight?"
" Fair Prince, believe my knightly word,
  I came not with free will;
I do confess that I have erred;
But, as old Montfort's schemes I've heard,
  I live to serve thee still.

v.

Within the Castle of Hereford,
Edward is under watch and ward.
The castle moat is wide and deep,
Gloomy and darksome is the keep,
  The battlements are high;
Young Edward is too proud to weep,
  Nor is he heard to sigh,
Yet pineth he for liberty,
  And passeth many a night

Devising plans to set him free,
And he cost his gaoler certainly
　　Many a taper light.

VI.

But guilty conscience cannot rest,
　　This Simon Montfort knows;
A thousand terrors fill his breast
　　Whene'er he seeks repose;
If slumber deign'd to close his eyes,
A thousand fearful dreams arise;
Asleep, awake, he is in dread
Lest the good Barons should make head
And rally in arms on field again,
To rescue their Prince and Sovereign:
The gates and doors are locked and barr'd,
At each is set a trusty guard,
And troopers armed for sudden fray
Scour the country night and day;
The castle battlements are mann'd
With choicest archers shaft in hand,

And woe be to the luckless wight
Who comes within a bowman's sight,
If he the password hath forgot,
Or to the warder answers not.

VII.

Yet Leicester thinks, " I'm belted Earl,
And must not bear me like a churl;
I know the deeds which I have done
Have angered many a baron's son.
The English yeomen love young Ned;
  And if he should get free,
I stand a chance to lose my head;
  'Twere better policy
To shew my royal birds respect;
I'll straitly charge my seneschal
To punish every menial
  Who dares to shew neglect."
So Edward hath a horse at need,
Though one but little famed for speed;
In the broad day-light he may ride—
With Leicester's troopers at his side;

And they are better armed I trow,
Sheathed in steel from top to toe ;
In faith, so strictly charged are they,
They might not even let him stay
To change a word with village lass,
  Nor e'en to bid good day,
Or ask how the dull hours may pass,
  If any crossed their way.

VIII.

Twelve months had run their weary race,
  Young Edward grieved at length ;
Youth little loves a narrow space,
When limbs are lithe and full of grace,
  And gathering in strength ;
When spirits mount as day awakes,
And when the buoyant fancy takes
O'er plain or mountain steep to rove,
  Or by some forest stream,
Where over-head the cushat dove
Sings to her mate soft notes of love ;
  Or falls the moonlight beam

In chequered rays upon the tide,
To watch the waters dance and glide ;
   Whilst inklings of love's dream
First waken in his wondering breast
   A stranger, with a boon
All kind, and deemed a welcome guest,
   Then wished away, how soon !
Or, if he be of English blood,
Loveth he not on ocean's flood
   In gallant bark to sail,
Braving the waves in angry mood,
   And e'en the roughest gale ?
No wonder then if Edward's cheek
   Hath worn a hectic shade
So long, and his dull eyes bespeak
   How the canker-worm hath preyed ;
And ever as he glanced his eye
   Beyond the waving hills
That formed his furthest boundary,
   That eye a tear-drop fills ;
Thought he, " Across yon' rolling stream,
   Beyond the forest-line,

Lives Roger Mortimer, I deem
 He is a friend of mine ;
I wot if he but knew my jail,
 There'd be a gathering
Of gallant lances bright in mail,
And banners flaunting in the gale,
 And war-shouts echoing ;
O ! for a chance when as a knight
I could do battle for my right
 Against this gaoler lord ;
Although he keepeth spy and scout
Within the castle and without,
 I'd stake it on my sword.

IX.

The river in his golden sheen
 Rolled past him merrily,
Whose banks were in their summer green,
On which innumerous flowers were seen
 In rich variety,

Such as shepherd-hinds would cull
  Their May-day Queen to prank,
And breathing odours sweet and full
  Along each mossy bank.
The merry songsters of the sky
Carolled their matins up on high;
The butterfly on wings of gold
  Was kissing every flower,
And though an arrant flirt of old
  And changeful as the hour,
The loveliest seemed offering
To the rover hearty welcoming;
All things that flaunted in the sun,
  Around him and below,
In frolic humour seemed to run,
  Nor had a tinge of woe.
So Edward to his chamber went,
His heart grew sick at merriment
  He saw and might not know;
If there he gave some anger vent,
'Twas but the uncurbed spirit's bent,
  Who else would not do so?

Little there was in that lone room
To cheer the prisoner in his gloom;
He looked out from his window light,
Its height forbade all hope of flight,
And if he saw the sunlit sky,
Or caught the perfumed zephyr's sigh,
Or heard the distant woods around
With sweetest melody resound––
All these but made him droop the more;
　The sunbeams as they threw
Their light upon his prison floor,
　Gave but a sickly hue
To the rich and costly tapestry
　Which hung around the walls,
Emblazoning in varied dye
Scenes that would glad a warrior's eye,
　In his own castle halls;
Gay tournaments and fierce mêlée,
And gallant knights in war's array,
　Or fairest ladies there,
Seemed grouped before him every day,
And as each hope fled fast away,
　They nourished his despair.

X.

In oaken seat the Prince reposed,
His eyes, in musing train he closed;
Then a deep and pleasant slumber crept
Upon him, and somewhile he slept;
" Fair Prince take thy full meed of rest,
And find the sorrow in thy breast

Is gone when thou shalt wake—"
Whose voice was that? What hidden guest

These cheering tidings spake?
Or did he dream? Upstarted he
As from some broken reverie,
He glanced his wondering eyes around,
A little scroll lay on the ground;
He searched the room with cautious fear
To see if Leicester's spies were near,
Then hastily he broke the seal,
His sparkling eyes good news reveal—

" To-morrow then! come quick, good morrow,
  And Leicester's bird is lost;
I shall no longer need to borrow
  My lodging at his cost;
And if Heaven grant we meet once more,
I'll soon rub off my gaoler's score."

XI.

The morrow came, it was a day
In that ever merry month of May,
And such a day it was indeed
As ever May-day Queen would need;
Ne'er looked the sun so glorious
  When rising from his sleep,
He took good leave of Erebus
  And burst upon the deep.
Aurora, when she caught his eye,
Blushed with a maiden's modesty,
When the lover of her heart
Tieth the knot man cannot part;

Loud echoed the far woods again
With one deep universal strain.

XII.

The castle Seneschal came down
With somewhat of an angry frown,
And said to a waiting menial,
As he passed through the warder's hall,
" Our Prince is in a hungry mood,
    Which is most strange to see ;
A venison pie before him stood,
' Certes,' says he, ' 'tis very good,'—
    He has left none for me :
A flagon of stout ale he quaffed,
    And asked me for another,
The which he finished in one draught,
    And called me his good brother."
Answered the other unto him,
" 'Tis well he is in such good trim ;
Last night, you know, it was agreed,
    To help the day along,

A match should be to try the speed
Of young Earl Gloucester's dark grey steed,
    A gallant one and strong;
So tell him at our castle-gate
His gay companions for him wait.
It seems to be the Earl's behest,
Whatever is his ward's request,
To have it done, he knoweth best,
But Edward hath a winning art,
    And many love him here
Who would be glad to take his part,
    If ever he got clear
From Leicester's keep; to thee or me
It matters little, as I see."

XIII.

The shrilly bray of clarion
    Now echoed in the court,
And woodland rangers one by one
    Rode from the Eastern port;

Next turned out the castle guard,
The Marshall ranged them on the sward,
To watch the movements of the day,
Fifty lances bold were they,
Cased in steel from head to foot,
With spear and battle-axe to boot.
The Marshal was of Leicester's kin,
    In treason deep had moved;
He was one the old Earl trusted in,
    For the Prince he little loved;
His old grey head, full well he knew,
    Would not be long his own,
And must pay for his crimes the forfeit due,
    When the King regained his throne.

XIV.

Young Edward came, a joyous smile
    Sparkled in his blue eyne,
All said that long had been the while
    Since one so bright did shine;

Then bowing to the Company,
" Fair greeting to ye all,"
Quoth he, " I deem it kind in ye,
To grace me with a call;
Last night, if I forget me not,
We all agreed to try a match
Between our steeds on yonder spot;
What saith the Marshal, that some plot
Against the state we hatch ?"
" Nay, Royal Prince, I should feel shame,
Were I to hinder such fair game ;
And more, I bet my baton's weight,
In silver or in gold,
That yon' grey steed will win the plate,
See here the stakes are told."
Said Edward, " I would gage my throne
On good Earl Gloucester's dapple roan."
Old Waldemar replied, " Fair Sir,
Earl Gloucester does not care to stir
As yet, and if we stay the sport
Until he comes, it will be short ;

I urge that we begin the race,
That is, if it so please your grace."
Prince Edward laughed, " What! Gilbert Clare
Still snoozing idly in his lair !
I thought our shouts would ring him up ;
   But, Gentles, ere we start,
Let each one drink in morning cup
   To the lady of his heart :
Yet will I wager even now
The Earl sings to his lady's brow,
Not rolling sluggishly in bed,
I know he hath a wiser head.

XV.

The sun was verging to the West ;
Every steed had done his best ;
The pace of each began to slack,
And his rider, lolling on his back,
Would doff his cap and wipe his brow,
And wish a cooling gale might blow.

Young Gilbert Clare stood listlessly
  Under the castle wall,
Sometimes gazing on the sky
  Or watching the shadows fall;
At times he trilled a merry strain,
  Or some old madrigal;
He held a charger by his rein,
Now pacing him upon the plain;
  'Twas the choicest steed of all;
He eyed old Waldemar askance,
  As if it crossed his mind
To send him on some idle dance,
  But fortune was not kind;
Thought he, " We e'en must trust to chance
  And other method find."
" Thou art a lazy one this morn,"
  Quoth Waldemar, " or else the horn
That rung so merrily and long,
Had broke thy sleep, however strong;
The Prince and those young gallants there
Seem homewards now at ease to bear,

Be not too quick to take offence,
They'll break a joke at thy expense,
Sluggards who like their beds so well
Are fitter for an old monk's cell,
And ne'er will win their way to fame,
Shame, Gilbert! Earl of Gloucester, shame!"
The young Earl laughed, made short reply,
And on the ground he cast his eye,
As if he thought the old man's word
Was not the falsest he had heard.

XVI.

Earl Gilbert's steed, as I am told,
　Shewed breeding choice and rare;
Nor was he easy task to hold,
　Whilst idle groom-boys there
Scanned head and neck and shoulder-plate,
　Examined eye and tooth;
Each sagely nodded to his mate,
　Well satisfied forsooth.
But when young Edward saw the steed,
Far deeper cause had he indeed

F

To feel delight : " Thou hast been kind,"
Thought he, " to keep thy nag behind :
I'll warrant there's no courser here
Could match his paces in a year."
" Wilt please you mount him, fair young sir,
    You will need neither rod nor spur,"
Said Gilbert Clare ; " a better one
Never had King to ride upon
    For battle or for chase ;
To leap a dyke, or stem a tide,
He hath no equal.   Will you ride
    And try his step and pace ?
And if, Sir Prince, he pleaseth thee,
Accept him as a boon from me,
    And thou wilt do me grace."
" Sir Gilbert, thou art all too kind ;
    We owe thee more than we can pay
E'en now, and if I were inclin'd,
    Our Marshal would say nay ;
For I may only use such flesh
    As Leicester's grooms get ready,
Who ne'er will let them be too fresh,

Though they are sure and steady.
But surely little harm will fall
   To try the courser here;
The guards are ready at his call,
   (They always are too near.)"
There was not one could think it wrong,
They deemed the castle guard too strong:
T'were madness to attempt a flight
Whilst the old Marshal was in sight.
So Edward smoothed his flowing mane;
   Looked at the saddle girth;
He paced him slowly on the plain
A little way, and back again;
   Then springing from the earth,
Leaped featly on the courser's back,
(Old Waldemar was on the rack;)
" I like his paces well indeed:
   Sir Marshal, may I try his speed?"
Old Waldemar looked darker still,
   Knitted his brows and frowned;
And yet he feared to shew ill will,
   So he turned quickly round

To give some order to his guards,
But the Prince had reached some hundred yards,
And looking back he waved his cap:
" Sir Marshal, you are on the nap,
    But farewell gentle sir,
To bring me back on Montfort's land,
The fleetest rider in your band
    Will find he needs his spur ;
And please thee, to the Earl rehearse
    That I have sorely grieved
To be such charge upon his purse,
    Which now he'll find relieved ;
My kindest thanks I pray ye give
    For his paternal care,
I will repay him if I live,
    With interest full and fair."

XVII.

" Ho! treachery !" the Marshal said,
  " Up archers to the tower,
Draw your cloth shafts to the head,
And he, I ween, who lays him dead,
    Will gain a lady's dower:

Troopers to your ranks advance,
Draw his good sword every lance;
And if he long can keep that speed
Swift must be his horse indeed."
Many a cloth-yard shaft was drawn,
But each fell harmless on the lawn;
The archers did not aim aright,
Perchance a sunbeam crossed their sight;
But some might think 'twas not the thing
To slay the son of England's King.
Old Hubert called the Eagle Eye,
 Who ne'er was known to miss his mark,
Whispered to those who stood him nigh,
 They might shoot in the dark,
For far had princely Edward got
Beyond the longest arrow shot,
" And 'twere not so, 'tis not my mood,
 Whilst I am in the craft,
That England's best and royal blood
 Should stain an English shaft."

XVIII.

Now martial sounds are echoing
    Under the castle-wall,
Where the armed troops were gathering
    To the shrill trumpet call;
For hot pursuit the word was given;
    Earl Leicester takes the lead;
Swift as the forked light of heaven
    Is each stout lance's speed:
Glance in the sunlight helm and spear,
    Young Edward looked behind,
As the clashing steel hath reached his ear
    Borne on the evening wind;
He heard the shout of Montfort's Lord
As he pointed to him with his sword:
"Take him alive, but if not, death!—"
    This was said in an underbreath.
Doth Edward's courser flag? Oh! no,
    He keeps both wind and pace;
All vainly yon' pursuing foe,
    May hope to win the chase;

He hath plunged into the rolling tide,
   He stemmed the current's force,
And he hath gained the steep bank side:
   God speed the gallant horse!
But oh! sad chance! whilst that brave steed
Still stoutly held his lightning speed,
   The saddle girths gave way,
With stunning force young Edward fell;
The foe improved their chance too well
   As on the ground he lay.

XIX.

" Yield thee, Sir Edward! yield or die!"
   Soon as he reached the spot,
Shouted old Leicester tauntingly:
   Said Edward, " I will not!
I am thy sovereign master's son;
   Thou art his vassal, Sir Earl,
Though ever a disloyal one,
False to thy oath of fealty,
Thou stain to knighthood's pure degree
   Which in thy teeth I hurl!

Thou hast good steel on front and back,
　　And on thy craven head,
This 'vantage thou canst see I lack
　　And am but poorly sped;
Yet never will I yield to thee,
Or one so stained with villainy,
　　So at thee perjured lord!
God and the Blessed Saints aid me,
　　And strengthen my arm and sword!"
" Now fair young Prince, thou needs must yield,"
　　Exclaimed some friendly voice,
" Without thy mail, or lance, or shield,
　　Thou canst not have a choice
Against such odds."　But on the wind
　　The warning voice was lost;
Edward was not in yielding mind,
　　And thrice his breast he cross'd;
He doffed his cap, and loosed his vest,
　　And drew his long steel brand,
He flung his scabbard to the west,
　　And firmly clenched his hand.

XX.

Thrice had they crossed each flashing blade,
 And thrice they struck again,
The desperate stroke each foeman made
 Scattered fire-sparks o'er the plain.
Edward, though bold and desperate,
 Yet stood upon his guard;
Old Montfort struck with mortal hate,
 And pressed his 'vantage hard;
Anon, a trumpet's distant sound
 Came faintly on the gale;
There was a pause, each looked around,
 And Leicester's cheek turned pale;—
Another blast, and louder still,
 And it seemed to come more nigh:
The echoes now were loud and shrill,
Whilst from the summit of yon' hill
 The rolling dust-clouds fly;
The heavy galloping of horse
 Thundered upon the plain,
The mingling clank of an armed force

Made Edward hope again,
For as the lingering sunbeams shone
On each lance-head and morion,
　O'er which a banner streamed,
By the rich blazoning thereon,
　'Twas Mortimer he deemed.

XXI.

That loyal Knight was in advance,
　His sword stretched to the foe,
And shouted as he couched his lance,
　" On to the rescue, ho !
Old Montfort tarry till I come,
I'll charge thy many treasons home,
　Or ne'er again meet foe."
Then to his charger's reeking sides
He gave the spur, and on he rides
　In haste to lay him low.
" Now Heaven be with thee, Mortimer,
　'Twill be a goodly feat,
If thou hast strength of arm to bear
　Yon' traitor from his seat."

The Earl of Leicester's brow grew black,
He reined his foaming steed aback
  As if the charge to meet;
But Mortimer had force too strong
  All armed in England's right;
The traitor knew himself in wrong,
  Which oft unnerveth might;
And so he did not ponder long
  If he should venture fight:
" Sir Roger Mortimer, I trow
Thou hast the better 'vantage now,
  I yield the Prince to thee;
To spill good blood will not be fair:
Perhaps 'tis time that England's heir
  Should have his liberty."

XXII.

Then many a joyous cheer, and strong
  The gallant lances raised;
And as the tidings spread along
  Bells rung and bonfires blazed

On England's village heaths, I ken,
    And in each merchant town,
For loyal hearts have Englishmen
    And faithful to the Crown,
When demagogue and infidel
    Will suffer them to rest,
Nor teach them doctrines false and fell,
    And deadly as a pest.

The Battle of Crecy,

1346.

The following Piece is merely an attempt to reduce to metre and rhyme a short sketch of the battle of Crecy, of which all Englishmen, who are not disciples of Elisha Burritt, may be somewhat proud. I have subjoined a short extract from "Froissart's Chronicles."

"The King afterwards ordered that the army should be divided into three battalions. In the first he placed the young Prince of Wales; and with him, the Earls of Warwick and Oxford, Sir Godfrey de Harcourt, and many other knights and squires whom I cannot name. There might be in the first division about eight hundred men-at-arms, two thousand archers, and a thousand Welshmen. In the second battalion were the Earls of Northampton and Arundel, and many others, amounting on the whole to about eight hundred men-at-arms, and twelve hundred archers. The third battalion was commanded by the King; and was composed of about seven hundred men, and two thousand archers."

The French army, according to Hume and other historians, consisted of one hundred and twenty thousand men.

The Battle of Crecy.

I.

ALL night on Crecy's field
 The English army lay;
Each warrior rested on his shield
 Until the breaking day;
And scarcely had the glimmering light
Glanced upon helm and armour bright,
 As the night-clouds rolled away,
When the clarion's shrill strain
Rang long and loudly o'er the plain;
 And from their grassy bed,
Uprose the bristling hosts amain,
Who, answering to the call again,
 To their several stations sped.

Anon the banner of England's King
　　Waved on the morning breeze,
As it were a herald summoning
All gallant hearts the land could bring,
　　Nor braver crossed the seas.

II.

As Warwick's Earl leaped on his steed,
　　He said unto his lances,
" My merry gentlemen, indeed,
　　We have but fearful chances;
Twice sixty thousand men in mail
　　Yon' King of France can muster;
But we of twenty thousand fail,
　　Tho' a right sturdy cluster
As ever buckled armour on,
　　And stood in battle trim.
·   The cup of honour to be won
　　Is full unto the brim."
" Now fear you nothing, good Sir Earl,
　　For our limbs are sound and tough

Ere the night-clouds again unfurl,
  Those French shall have enough :
Of right true English blood are we,
  And tho' not given to boast
As.those gay lords of Gascony,
  Not one will quit his post."
Answered Earl Warwick, " Gallant hearts,
  Fear never soiled my breast ;
I doubt not ye will do your parts,
  Kind Heaven will do the rest."

III.

The chivalry of France
  Moved on in glittering show ;
Whilst in hot haste the ranks advance
  To battle with the foe :
Nought could the eye behold,
  Save myriads of glancing spears,
And banner-flags of silk and gold ;
As each high Lord his own unrolled,
  Uprose his vassals' cheers.

King Philip's blood began to boil
   His ancient foe to see
Arrayed so firmly on his soil;
   He shouted lustily:
" Lord Marshal, lead those bowmen on;
   Let them begin this fight;
Lead forwards in God's name anon,
   St. Denis for our right!"

IV.

Lord Warwick heard that battle shout
   As to the skies it rose;
Said he, " We must keep sharp look out
   Upon our bustling foes;
For see, how Count Alençon rides,
   And spurs his charger's flanks;
The red blood welters from his sides;
Hark ye ! how wrathfully he chides
   Yon' bowmen to their ranks;
They fit their quarrels to the bow;
   Now some of us must fall;

(Though weary hands they seem, and slow,)
   And Heaven assoilzie all!
Thanks to the Virgin! ne'er a shaft
   Hath even scratched our mail;
I'll wager for our English craft
   Not one of ours shall fail.
But long enough we've stood the brunt,
   They soon shall taste our yew;
Up merry archers to the front,
   Be steady and pull true."

v.

In darkening showers thick and fast
   The English arrows fell;
And each as it flew whizzing past
   Sounded a Frenchman's knell.
The Genoese in sore dismay
   From that dread storm recoil'd,
The men-at-arms behind gave way,
Many a lord all gasping lay
   In his harness all besoil'd.

But still came that unerring flight,
Death following in grim delight;
Every shaft the fiend bestrode
Laughing as the life-stream flow'd;
And the shrieks of the dying rent the skies
As they writhed in their last agonies.

VI.

Alençon's spirit groaned in wrath,
  As knight and charger sank
In crowds beneath that deadly math,
Whose welt'ring bodies choked his path
  And thinned each battle rank.
Shouted he, with thundering voice,
"Laggards and dolts is this your choice
  To stand beneath these showers;
One gallant charge must drive these men
Back to their English shores agen,
  And the victory shall be ours."
Plunging the rowels in his steed,
Onwards he charged with desperate speed.

Uprose the war-shout of each Lord;
  Pealed high the trumpet strain;
Every vassal unsheath'd his sword,
  And gave his steed the rein;
The clang of steel and tramp of horse,
As rank on rank charged on in force,
  Made earth to shake again.

VII.

With anxious look Alençon gazed
  On every blazoned shield,
On crested helm, and banner raised
  Above that stormy field:
Thought he, that Boy of English pride
  I've sworn I will chastise;
Where doth the stripling warrior hide?
'Tis said not sixteen summers' tide
  Hath he yet seen to rise;
If I should meet him in mêlée,
'Twould be but little more than play;
  No feat for me to prize."

On, on ! ye flowers of chivalry !
　　On, Gentlemen of France,
Let each one think his lady's eye
　　Beholds her own true lance.
But mark, bring sudden word to me
　　If any meet young Ned ;
I've sworn this day that I or he
　　Shall here find his death-bed."—
" Thou speakest truly, boasting Count,
　　Choose here thy place of rest ;
But first of all with Walter Blount
　　Thou needs must do thy best.
Fifty Knights, and I am one,
　　Have sworn on point of sword,
No harm shall reach King Edward's son,—
　　Not one will fail his word."
The warriors met with desperate shock,
　　The gallant Walter fell ;
Alençon sat him like a rock
　　Amidst the tempest's swell ;
" Twas a brave stripling, by my faith,
　　Bright eyes will weep to-night,

Should thy fair ladye see thy wraith
  All in the pale moon-light."
And then the vaunting warrior
  Waved his sword over head;
Spurring his gallant steed once more,
  He leaped him o'er the dead.
" On, for St. Denis !" and he rushed
  To the hottest of the fray;
It seemed for a while the din was hushed
  Wherever he made his way :
He fought as it were with giant's strength;
On the ground each one measured his length
  Who dared his course to stay.

VIII.

Meanwhile King Edward watched the fray;
His men-at-arms around him lay;
And sorely grieved it many a Knight,
Who saw the progress of the fight,
To sit upon his mettled steed
In idleness when warlike deed

And feats of arms were to be done,
And knightly honour to be won ;
And ever as the clamour rose,
And fled or charged again the foes,
Or English war-cry reach'd the ear,
" St. George ! a Warwick ! or De Vere !"
Or fiercer grew the battle din,
'Twas hard to rein each war-horse in.

IX.

Cried Edward, " Look ye, gallant sirs,
  A Knight pricks hitherward :
Methinks, he useth those gilt spurs
  Much better than his sword.
" Sir Thomas Norwich ! Is it well?
  Why have ye left the field ?
What news ? What news have ye to tell ?
  My Britons do not yield ?"
" Dread Sovereign, your Englishmen
Will never yield one inch I ken
  Whilst life and limbs do last ;
Right steadily they keep their ground,

But still the foemen press around
   In numbers thick and fast;
The Germans, forty thousand strong,
   Hem in the Prince's corps;
They cannot bide the struggle long
   With only half a score:
Then Philip of Valois is prest
   With thirty thousand more,
Who all the while have been at rest,
   On our thin ranks to pour.
Our men act wonders; ne'er can tongue
   Do justice to each feat;
But Sire, full sure their knells are rung,
   Unless thou thinkest mete
To lead thy warriors to aid. .
   Oh! all that can be done
Is done; and many a knight is laid,
Who ne'er again with spear or blade
   His martial course will run."

G

X.

"How fares it with our Boy, Sir Knight?
    Is he alive and sound?
For if he be unscathed and right,
    I will not quit this ground."
"My liege! thy noble son is well,
    Right bravely hath he foughten.
De Blois beneath his young arm fell—
But time would fail me now to tell
    The deeds which he hath wroughten.
And if it be thy will, he saith,
    He'll fight the battle out
Alone, if Heaven will grant him breath,
Nor will he budge an inch till death
    Shall stop his battle-shout."
"Then good Sir Thomas, tell my son
    That I did roundly swear,
This battle should be solely won
By those who have so well begun;
    And they alone shall wear

The honor, who so valiantly
  Have toiled through strife and heat:
So back, Sir Thomas, and from me
  Most kindly each one greet;
And say that Heaven, full well I know,
  Will shine upon our right:
Now, do your doing on the foe,—
  Farewell, my trusty Knight."

XI.

Sir Thomas reached the battle plain:
  " What says our Sovereign Lord?"
Cried Warwick, as he paused again,
  And wiped his streaming sword.
" He saith he will not quit his post;
  And swears his son shall earn
His spurs, whatever be the cost;
  But those around him burn
To run a course and deal a blow,
  And think it shame to sit
In idleness so near a foe;
  Much grumble they at it."

The gallant Prince of Wales then rose
　　High in his saddle-seat;
He ope'd his visor, bared his brows,
　　To cool their burning heat;
How proud he was you all might see
　　When his Father's message came,
For in the lists of chivalry,
There was not a braver Knight than he
　　With a brighter or purer name;
" Gallants! our royal Sire is kind;
　　We are indeed much graced :
Now, by St. George, he shall not find
　　His trust in us misplaced ;
Are any here of sickly mood,
　　Or wishful to depart,
Or one that fears to look on blood,—
For a sword in the hand is little good
　　If there be an unwilling heart?"
Better for such to speed away,
Ere we who are sound resume our play;
　　He hath our leave to start."

XII.

But it seemed as if new hearts were stirr'd,
When each King Edward's message heard;
More fiercely then the battle raged : .
The English chivalry engaged,
  Some two, some three, some four;
With desperate energy all fought,
And mighty feats indeed were wrought,
As to the charge fresh foes were brought
  Against the English corps.
Charge after charge the Frenchmen led,
But left a towering pile of dead;
Many a chieftain's banner fell,
Whose silken folds no more would swell
In blazon'd pride upon the gale,
There left for foemen's hand to trail
In dust and gore along the earth ;
Many a youth of noble birth,
Whose soul, as glanced that morning's sun
His polish'd shield and casque upon,

Was mounting with chivalric fire,
Dreaming ere night to tell his Sire
What feats had graced his maiden shield,
Lay stiffening on the battle-field.
Fortune had darkly lowered on France,
In vain her countless lines advance,
In vain each Lord his vassals cheer'd,
In vain the Oriflamme upreared
Her ample folds of gold and red,
The Lilies of fair France were dead:
Around and o'er them hovering,
Screamed raven birds of evil wing,
So deemed, at least in wizard's lore,
Disheartening many a warrior.

XIII.

Old Luxenbourg sat on his steed,
    And with his harness on;
His dim grey eyes roll'd quick indeed,
    Their sight had long been gone:
" How fares the battle noble Lords
    To us, or ill or well?"

" Oh ! Sire, we have but evil words
   Indeed as yet to tell.
No longer stout Alençon cries,
   ' St. Denis ! à la France !'
Beneath his banner-flag he lies,
Closed in death are his fierce eyes,
   Shent are his sword and lance.
D'Aumale hath fall'n, and breathed his last,
   De Blois and brave Lorraine ;
Tho' loud may speak the trumpet blast,
   They ne'er will rise again."
" Brave Lords and Vassals, ye are all
   Companions old in fight,
Come, lead me now where I may fall
   As best becomes a Knight."
That ancient King they gathered round,
   And one on either side
Their bridle-reins in his then wound,
   And linked together ride,
Full in the thickest of the strife
   Charged that devoted band—
Not one came out again with life,—
   Not one had sheathed his brand.

XIV.

King Philip grasped his good sword hilt,
  And flung his scabbard down :
" To live would now be fearful guilt,
  When so much noble blood is spilt,
    I'll perish with my crown."
Count Hainault seized his bridle rein,
  " Oh Sire, I pray not so ;
All valour now would be in vain,
'Twere best to quit this fatal plain,
  And live to meet our Foe
Some other day, when better chance
  May even yet be ours ;
Remember still our merry France
  Hath raised but half her powers.
Come, Sire, away ! whilst yet thy steed
  Thy royal weight can carry ;
'Twill try e'en now his speed and wind,
Some resting-place this night to find,
  Where we may safely tarry."

XV.

The light of day declined apace,
Night rolled her clouds o'er Heaven's face,
And lesser grew the battle yell
As banner after banner fell;
Each charge grew fainter and more slack,
And many failed in the attack:
Whilst in the thickening veil of night
Many a one turned from the fight,
Where panic raged in fearful sway,
And rushed in wild despair away;
Then by degrees the clamour sank
And died away; a heavy clank
Told when the last mailed warrior
Had fallen; the battle raged no more,
And loudly cheered each English son,
When the mighty victory was won.

XVI.

"Listen, brave Knights," said England's King,
  "By my faith that's a British shout:
They have won the day, let the welkin ring
  With an echo long and stout.
Now Sirs, we will forward to meet our Son:"
  And hastily on rode he,—
"My Boy! my Boy! thou hast nobly done!
  And my noble British hearts, each one
    Hath quitted him valiantly."
The young Prince lighted from his steed,
  And kneeled down on the ground:
"Father, we've foughten with good speed,
  First with all thanks to Heaven indeed,
    Then to my comrades around."
King Edward's cheeks were moist with joy;
  He strained to his heart his gallant Boy:
"Thou art a Plantagenet I own,
  Right worthy thou of England's throne."

Charles II.

The following piece is intended as a sketch of three passages in the life of Charles II.

Charles II.

" MOURNFULLY, mournfully,
     Whistle the night winds over me !
These melancholy gales
Seem to me as the wails
  For my lost majesty.
Why was I born
  In royal pride and power,
To be an outcast most forlorn,
  Forsaken in my needful hour ?
It is young Autumn now,
Whose breath should cool my burning brow ;
But yet the very elements
  Methinks are leaguers with my foes ;

And, whilst these slumber in their tents,
  And take their sweet repose,
Keep up continuous war and strife,
To crush, or wear away my life.
Dark clouds are sweeping o'er the arch
  Of the incensed Heaven,
Like troopers on their march
  To whom is given
License to desolate at will
Each smiling vale and rich crowned hill:
The very thunder speaks in wrath
  Against such parricidal deeds;
The forked lightning marks a path
  Where the avenger leads ·
His ministers to overwhelm
This miserable realm."

II.

In ragged garb and clouted shoon
  The Royal Wanderer traced his way
Through the dark forest, star and moon
  Withheld their friendly ray;

And well they might, for evil powers
   Ran riot through the land,
Whose deeds were meet for darkest hours;
   And many a godless band
Were scouring upland, lowland glen,
Woodland, glade, and distant fen,
   Island, and rock and strand,
In eager haste and thirsty mood
For one more drop of royal blood.

III.

" I faint, I faint,
   From my heart's very weariness!
Oh martyr'd Saint!
   My Father! canst thou bless
Thine outcast Son,
Driven from his old paternal halls,
And dare not bide in cottage walls:
Whom each must shun,
Because 'tis death to see
   And not betray
To his blood-thirsty enemy;
   I faint, would it were day!

Yet what will daylight bring to me?
   The merry lark may wing
Up to the Heavens upon the breath
   Of balmy scented Spring;
But I must cower beneath,
   Like any guilty thing.
Hist! some one passes; 'tis the tramp
Of warrior from rebel camp:
Be darker, darkest night,
Or else put out my life's own light,
For feeble is its lamp.
'Tis past; again I am alone,
My heart sits lighter on its throne;
And see, the day already breaks
Along the skies in golden streaks."

IV.

At last in flood of glorious sheen,
   The majesty of Heaven forth sailed;
Up soared into the Heavens serene
   The merry lark, and hailed
His brother choristers, to wake
On every dew bespangled brake;

And sweet and loud that matin-song
Caroll'd forth by the feather'd throng,
Whose rich melodious strains deep sank
 Into that fugitive's sad breast,
As on the perfum'd green turf bank
 His aching feet to rest
He laid him down.   But short the grace
He had to rest from weary race;
For soon the ring of charger's foot,
And distant trumpet-call to boot,
Warned him the foe was passing near;
The sounds came nearer, and his ear
Could mark the words of import dread:
" A thousand pounds upon his head!
We've followed hard upon his rout,
He must be somewhere hereabout."

v.

" Where shall I hide?
 These limbs are all too tired to save;—
Oh! Earth, my mother, open wide
 .And cover me in kindly grave—

Or shall I fight, and die,
　　Like gallant knight of old;
'Twere better than to yield, and lie
In dungeon dark and cold:—
Yet, on the topmost bough, perchance,
　　Of yon' magnificent oak tree,
May be they will not think to glance
　　Up there for me;
Up higher—now another yet;—
　　Peace, and be still my heart!
Under this tree the files are met,
　　Each one to tell his part.
They little guess how near is he,
Whose head its worth in gold would be.
They heed me not—but sit beneath,
　　And fill their horns with cheer so good,
Spiced with the perfumes of the heath;
　　Drink of it heartily I could,
　　For it is long since I took food.
Now thanks to Heaven all merciful!
　　They go and I am safe once more;
The storm within me is at lull,
　　And I may reach the shore."

VI.

Another footstep on the ground!
But now it falls with lighter sound
Than soldier's foot, the step is free;
And hither comes across the lea,
Some peasant in whose open face
I can at least kind spirit trace.
Methinks I know those features well;
Surely 'tis Arthur Penderell!
A friend more staunch unto the death
Never had monarch who drew breath.
"My Royal Master!" "Nay, arise!
Thou knowest me in this disguise!
Must I command thee? Rise, my friend!
It is not here thy knee should bend;
No regal crown is on my brow,
Nought am I but Charles Stuart now."
"Oh! good my liege, I cannot brook
To see thy sad and haggard look,
He ill deserves an English name,
Who will not bend to thee the same

Whether thou art on England's throne
   Circled in pomp and power,
Or wandering sadly and alone
In poverty's dark hour.
That I have found thee, glad am I,
For there are good friends watching nigh;
Although the round-head troopers came
   To search my cottage on the bourne
Of this wide forest; sword and flame
   They threatened me this very morn,
(Their leader was fell Hambleton,)
If I should harbour Stuart's Son.
They promised me a guerdon rare,
If I would sell them England's heir;
But now we shall be free awhile;
And until better days do smile,
In safety may my liege abide
In my poor cottage, whilst I ride
To loyal Wilmot's lord; 'twill cheer
His heart, that thou art well to hear;
And God will help us whilst we plan
How we can shield thee from that man

Whose hand will ne'er be clean again
From the blessed Martyr's life-blood stain.

*   *   *   *

VII.

Gallantly, gallantly,
Over the bright waves of the sea
Glides yonder bark and bears away
Him for whom loyal hearts will pray.
Deep prayers were breathed for thee,
    Thou royal fugitive,
    That thou might'st live
Until a nation's voice and might
    Hurling the rebels down,
Give back thy own birthright,
    Thine own ancestral Crown !
God speed thee, gallant bark !
    God shield the Martyr's son
From traitors' guile and treasons dark
    Until their woof be spun !
And o'er the waves the vessel sped,
And many a loyal tear was shed,

As the young Charles waved last farewell.
Little was said, but you may tell
By the language of the eye
Where the deepest sorrows lie ;
Their hearts grew sadder as the trace
Of their hopes was lost on ocean's face ;
They wended homeward and each one,
Moved silently, and mused alone—

VIII.

Well might the generous and free
Weep o'er the page of History,
To read the names of Priest and Peer
And loyal-hearted Cavalier,
Who deemed their wealth no sacrifice,
Nor forfeit life too great a price
For England's Holy Church and laws,
Her sainted Monarch's rights and cause,
And swelled the tide of loyal blood
Shed in the nation's frenzied mood.
Upon the martyr-roll full high
Stands noble Strafford's name,

The good old Laud whose fearless eye
  No headsman's axe could tame ;
Earl Derby, King of Mona's Isle,
Lord Capel, Lucas, gallant Lisle,
And Scotland's glorious Montrose
Whose dauntless spirit loftier rose,
Though the wild puritanic hate
Gave noble blood to felon's fate.

    *   *   *   *   *   *

IX.

  Merrily, merrily,
The church bells echo chimes of glee ;
Banners stream from high church towers ;
Arches of the rich May-flowers,
  Culled by the fairest hands,
Are reared in rustic lanes,
And village streets, and plains.
  Along the road, were bands
Of well-dressed burghers, cavaliers,
Surpliced priests, and noble peers,
Gather in proud array ;
And 'prentice boys all gay

Are hastening down
From city and from town,
As on some holiday.

X.

The May-sun is in heaven's high arch,
  The winds are fair and free,
Yon' bark glides on in stately march
  Over the glassy sea;
Gay banners from her top-mast float;
  Upon her deck there stand
A group of men who seem of note,
  The high-born of the land.
And what rich argosy hath she,
  That every English eye
Is gazing there so fixedly,
  And each heart beating high?
Whilst stately lords, and yeomen brave
  Crowd down unto the beach,
And to the margent of the wave,
  As far as eye can reach;

Fair maidens' eyes are filled with tears,
  Not dimm'd with sorrow's leaven;
And yon' grey-headed cavaliers
  Raise thankful eyes to Heaven.
" He comes, he comes, oh happy day!
  Our deep loved, long lost King,
To take his own again, for aye,
  With a nation's welcoming!

X.

With thankful heart and joyous bound,
  Charles stepped along the plank,
And stood upon his native ground
  Erect in kingly rank:
Old Earls, and burghers, yeomen bold,
  Each on his bended knee,
Tendered their homage as of old;
  'Twas a glad sight to see,
As up unto the flagstaff-head
  On Dover's castle high,
The Royal Standard rose, and spread
  Her broad folds to the sky;

Then twice ten thousand voices pour
  Their cheerings loud and long,
And echoed to the cannon's roar
  That burst above the throng.
Brave Monk! proud thoughts must overwhelm
  Thy loyal heart that day,
Thou broughtest back old England's realm
  To her rightful monarch's sway,
And saw each sterling English heart
  Gush forth in loyalty;
I would that I had borne a part
  In such high jubilee.

MINOR POEMS.

Runnimede.

— ❖ —

THE Barons of our fair free land,
　　Each with his harness on,
Grasping the buckler, lance, and brand,
　　To Runnimede are gone.

Above their heads their banners float,
　　Swords in the sunlight flashing;
Uprose the trumpet's stirring note,
　　And the heavy arms were clashing.

John turned his dark and fiery eye
　　Upon those sturdy lords;
They quailed not from its scrutiny,
　　As they rested on their swords.

And then he turned his eye away,
　　For his heart within was cold,
To see their firm and brave array,
　　Their bearing free and bold.

For they were gathered there, he knew
  For merry England's right;
Their hearts were strong as oak, and true
  And dauntless in the fight.

Then stept the Earl Fitzwalter forth,
  And due obeisance rendered;
John's spirit in him waxed wrath,
  As a parchment-scroll he tendered.

Said he, " Why are my Barons met ?
  And what is it they need ?"
" My Liege we crave of thee to set
  Thy seal unto this deed."

John took the deed, he looked behind,
  His Brabançons were there ;
He knew them faithless as the wind,
  And groaned in his despair.

And then he watched those Lords again ;
  Amongst them all, thought he,
It may be I can lay some train
  For feud or jealousy.

But no, each feud aside was laid,
   Forgotten every broil;
For each had sworn on his sword's blade
   All lawless schemes to foil.

Then John, when he affixed his seal,
   Returned it to them proudly;
The doughty Barons clashed their steel,
   And shouted long and loudly.

'Twas thus those famous Lords of yore
   Stood for the common weal;
When John had stained his hands with gore,
   His Nephew's crown to steal.

And if the boon our Barons won
   Our Commons ere forget,
Too soon, I fear, our England's Sun
   In infamy will set.

Queen Elizabeth at Tilbury Fort.

—◆—

OUR Maiden Queen is on her steed,
    In glittering steel bedight ;
And troops are raised for England's creed
    And every Briton's right.

All gallantly she looked in arms,
    And wondered every Lord,
No woman's fear her heart alarms
    As she unsheathed her sword.

The English Burghers cheered again
    To see their own loved Queen
Ride like a warrior on the plain,
    With voice and brow serene.

" My loving people, I am come
    To share a soldier's toil ;
With ye to guard our English home
    From Popish chain and spoil.

" If Heaven so will to shed my blood,
  (Lay ease and pleasure down,)
Aye ! in the battle's heat and flood
  Ere stain my English Crown.

" I claim it through a famous race
    Of kingly warriors ;
  Ne'er shall Elizabeth disgrace
    Her gallant ancestors.

" Unfurl, unfurl our England's Flag !
    And rally underneath ;
  Whilst flutters to the breeze one rag
    Let sword not rest in sheath.

" Be all for one and one for all
    Linked in our sacred cause,
  The peasant's cot, the baron's hall,
    The throne, our church, and laws.

" Ye all are hearts of oak I ween,—
    All brave and free and true ;
  Right proud am I to be the Queen
    Of such a fearless crew.

" Soon as the Spanish thunder rolls
   Along our English shore,
Rouse up the lion in your souls
   As ye have done of yore.

" And there your Maiden Queen will ride,
   Nor shun the battle strife—
The first to plunge in its red tide,
   The last to quit with life.

" For if I have a woman's hand,
   My blood flows from a King;
And kingly thoughts my heart hath mann'd
   To think it hath its spring

" From those whose daring deeds of old
   Have filled the wide earth's spheres,
Plantagenet, the Lion bold,
   And Edward of Poictiers."

Shouted the English yeomen then :
   " Before high Heaven we vow,
As we are all true Englishmen,
   Our knees shall never bow

" Beneath a foreign tyrant's chains :
    Ere Spanish feet shall tread
As conquerors upon our plains
    Our life's last drop we'll shed.

" But come the Spaniard when he may,
    And strong as ere he can,
To drive them back will be mere play
    To any Englishman."

Young England.

—◆—

A CRY is gone from North to South: we
  want a master mind,
To cure the social ills which like a pestilential
  wind
Are sweeping o'er our merry land, all we love best
  to blast;—
God! hear us in our woful plight, and send us
  help at last!

Our Church which should be unity, and peace
  and love to all,
With sore divisions rent in twain, seems ready
  now to fall:
Tractarians, and Catholics, and Churchmen High
  and Low,
Are names which should be never heard, and
  cause her children woe.

They say the march of intellect should change
    our Church's rules,
And those who think these should not change are
    bigoted and fools;
Those who are set to teach the Faith, by their
    own Flock are taught:
The Sheep against the Shepherd rail; the good
    Priest set at naught.

With wealth unbounded in the land, of death from
    want we hear;
We boast we have the Gospel light, as from all
    error clear;
We scorn the Church of Rome because she wor-
    ships stone and wood;
Yet worship Mammon ever as the only source of
    good.

Tho' thousands perish daily for the lack of Gospel
    lore,
Fresh schemes are ever set on foot to encrease
    our golden store;
We cry unto our Governors to help us spread
    the light;
They seem to aid the wrong alone, and will not
    help the right.

We've seen the good old Tories merge within a
　　motley crew;
Conservatives they call themselves, but who'll
　　believe them true
To English rights and English laws, which they
　　have frittered down,
And seem alike indifferent to Poor, or Church, or
　　Crown.

They talk now of Young England, and if Young
　　England be
A true son of Old England there be none so good
　　as he:
Far better keep the good old stock and tread the
　　good old ways,
Than the false and empty doings of these change-
　　ful latter days.

Berechurch.

I KNOW a little hallowed spot,
   Where stands with ivy trophies crowned,
A lonely church like one forgot
   By all the world around.

A few tall trees there are which throw
   A chequered light and shade o'er those
Who sleep within the soil below
   In undisturbed repose.

The quiet Churchyard guarded off
   From yonder park with lowly fence,
Sends man who came perchance to scoff
   With better feelings thence.

Close by the fabric, rears its head
   A noble Oak, so brave a tree,
With sturdy arms wide overspread,
   You will not often see.

I said : That oak is England's pride,
  Meet emblem of her gallant race :
And yon' old Church which stands beside
  In venerable grace,

The mother from whose bosom runs
  The hallowed stream which warms their hearts,
Nerving the arms of her free sons
  And holier gifts imparts.

It seemed as if that ancient pile
  Stood under his protecting care ;
And glad my spirit felt the while
  I watched and pondered there.

'Tis meet, I thought, that every hand
  Should now be ready like yon' oak
To guard the churches of our land
  From foe or tempest stroke.

There are, I am not one of them,
  Who hold our Church in light esteem,
And thirst to pluck away each gem
  Which shed its hallowed gleam

Upon our land, and sends afar
    Its blessings o'er the distant main
To other regions where the star
    Reflects her light again.

There are who glad would see her fall
    Beneath the shock of time and foes,
Unmindful of the sacred call
    With which her bosom glows.

Walton le Soken.

—◆—

WHERE are the joyous days we spent
  Upon these sunny shores,
When friendship, love, and mirth were blent,
And each one on his several bent .
  Would open up rich stores
To help old Father Time along
With revelry or plaintive song?
Where are they we were wont to meet—
  Young forms from Beauty's bowers,
Smiling with summer looks as sweet
  And lovely as the flowers
That flourish on the breath of Spring,
Who seemed like graces wandering
Over the cliffs that girt the sea,
  Along the sands where every wave
Seemed echoing in jubilee
  With the sea-nymphs in their cave?

Ah hah! Old Ocean, was it not
  A joyous sight indeed,
To see a group in some wild spot,
  Sit down to take their feed
On benches rudely formed around,
A neat white cloth spread on the ground,
With plenty eye and taste to cheer,
And with a jug of stout old beer,
Beneath the bright blue canopy
Of Heaven, we quaffed a health to thee?

And now there's many a pleasant spot
  But for thy magic hand,
Oh Memory! would be forgot,
  Lies underneath yon' sand;
For I have heard my mother say,
  (Heaven's blessings on her head,)
That well she recollects the day
When, where the ocean waves now play
  Over the sandy bed,
The old grey parish church once reared
  Its venerable roof,

Where Gospel messages were heard
   For comfort and reproof.
One Sabbath morn the preacher stood
   And often stretched his eye
Along the ocean's swelling flood,
   Or watched the darkening sky;
For ever and anon burst forth
   The soughing of the North-West gale;
When it blows strongly from the North
   The old wives' cheeks turn pale;

Yet darker grew the clouds around,
The sullen breakers spoke a sound
Foreboding strife 'twixt wind and wave,
And the fierce shout the tempest gave
Quelled many a heart though stout and brave,
   And then the storm awoke;
The wide sea was a yawning grave
   As the huge surges broke
And rolled tumultuously on:
Shore, cliff, the old church-yard were gone—
And ne'er within those walls again
   Was heard the psalm or prayer;

The murmurs of the heaving main
   Alone resounded there.

Deep buried in the womb of time
   Those days are now, and hushed the song,
That echoed once so sweet a chime;
   And many a one of that bright throng
   Once scrambling these tall cliffs among,
   Is calmly slumbering
In the dark silent vault of death;
   And still on noiseless wing
The arch destroyer hurrieth
All pleasant days into the deep
And boundless ocean where they sleep,
Never to wake again; whilst I
   Remain, perchance the only one
To roam amongst the scenes, and sigh
   For those before me gone,
Yet dear to memory.

A Ramble.

——◆——

THIS is no night to sit within
  Poring o'er crabbed books
And dusty papers; 'tis a sin
  When with such winning looks
The Moon peers from her throne above,
This is a meeter hour to rove.

I donned my hat and rushed into the street—
  This din of rattling cars
Is to my ears but little treat;
  Besides it mars
The present humour of my mind,
Though it be changeful as the wind.

I sought the silver flood
  Tracing her course through meadows green,
Whose little waves in wanton mood
  Danced in the moonlight sheen.

The fields had late been bright with flowers
  · Where daisy and the lady cup
Assembled all their brilliant powers,
    And as the kine came out to sup
On these my favourites of old,
    I grieved to see they spared not one
Which I so loved, because they told
    Of days bygone,
When as a merry romping boy
    I culled those simple flowers to braid
Garlands and coronals for joy
    And deck some favourite maid;
E'en in those very childish days
    A maiden form would often come
To whom my stripling heart would raise
    A shrine within its home.

I felt the love shaft, and the power
    Of silvery voice, and witching smile;—
The wounds are gone, but to this hour
    My memory steals awhile

To many a form whose infant grace
   The child's light fancy captive led,
And still she haunts each charmed place
   Where the young heart first bled.

But hark! there is a distant sound
   Of music in yon' wood;
I heard it on all sides around,
   And spirit-chained I stood:
The carols of that little bird,
   Void of finesse and art—
Sweeter and richer are ne'er heard—
   Speak volumes to the heart.

The Moon was in her course above,
   A beauty reigning peerlessly
Amidst the glittering ranks of love,
   And such was she.
Red Mars, in all his warlike sheen,
   Stood near her silvery car,
Paying meet homage to the Queen,
   Yet were his thoughts afar;

For the chaste maiden stood between
   Him and his lady love,
Bright Venus, who near Earth was seen
   With witching looks to move;
Oh! with what matchless light she shone
   Amidst the lesser stars of heaven!
To none, save to my love's eyes alone.
   Such lustre hath been given.

"THE BEGINNING OF SORROWS."

OH! Holy Mother Church!
    When will these fierce divisions cease?
Where may thy faithful children search
    For thy best gifts of peace?
Shouldst thou, enduring for awhile
    The chastisement for sin
Of careless sons, and sons of guile
    Mingling thy fold within,
Be rent with this unhallowed broil
    Now raging in thy heart,
And yielded as a goodly spoil
    For eager foes to part?

Oh! whither shall we turn
    With weary step and tearful eye,
Whilst our sad hearts do yearn
    For blessed unity?

Not to the blood-stained hills of Rome,
　Though now, perchance, with milder voice,
She calls her former children home;—
　This may not be our choice,
Whilst her unwholesome lore
　Still taints her Church and hides the light,
And Gospel truths are hidden o'er
　With superstitious rite.

Along the dreary waste,
　Behold are Schism's hydra-heads
Leading her followers in rash haste
　Wherever self-will treads;
E'en here idolatry,
　Though in more subtil guise,
Erects her altars stealthily,
　Whilst Mammon blinds their eyes:
And sadder still to tell,
　Bold Infidelity awakes
To spread around her baneful spell,
　Whilst Faith's foundation shakes.

No Sacraments of Grace are here,
　Vigil, nor day of fast,
To draw the penitential tear
　For sins and errors past;
No Heaven-commissioned Priest to lead
　The daily round of prayer,
The Faith to teach, the Word to read,
　To seal Heaven's infant heir;
No festival, nor holy day,
　When hearers may be told
Of Saints who trod the Heavenward way,—
　Of high events of old.

Not here, then, may we rest;
　But from these forms and creeds unsound
We turn away as fails each test,
　And sadly gaze around
For shelter 'midst the strife,
　And fix our wistful glances back
On our loved Church which gave us life,
　Now but a mournful wrack :—

Not so, a holy pledge is given,
　　She standeth on a Rock;
In vain her foes around have striven,
　　She may defy the shock.
" The gates of Hell shall not prevail,"—
　　Cheer up thou drooping soul,
Her Saviour's promise will not fail,
　　Fierce as the storms may roll.

The Fall of Adam.

I.

FAIR to the eye, and sweet to taste,
    Gifts promised, too, of wondrous power!
Eve seized the fruit with trembling haste
    And sought the spousal bower,
Where, when the morning breeze first broke
    The silence of the moonlit night,
And every bird with song awoke
    To greet the burst of light,
She left her Mate, their first repast
    'Midst Eden's unforbidden stores
At will to seek; her eye upcast
    To those æthereal shores
Where dwelt the Messengers of Heaven
    Watching the new created pair,
To whom the Almighty God had given
    His choicest gifts and rare:

Free from all guilt she tripped along,
   Through flowering mead and tuneful grove,
Her young heart pouring out in song
   Its gratitude and love
To Him whose works of power and skill
   Shone in the earth, and seas, and skies,
And rose, as yet unstained by ill,
   Before her wondering eyes.

II.

Sad contrast now, as she returned
   With heavy step and slackened pace,
No more her buoyant spirit yearned
   To meet her husband's face
With smiles and welcome radiant;
   Over her heart crept feelings strange,
Like mildew o'er the healthful plant,
   And shuddered at the change;
Those wandering eyes which late had vied
   With the young planet's beauteous light,
Now sought each guilty glance to hide
   In the deep shades of night.

The song of bird ceased suddenly;
  Withered each lovely flower away;
The first storm hurtled in the sky;
  The first cloud veiled the day;
And who shall tell what sounds of grief
  Echoed amidst the angelic host,
When Eve first plucked the fatal leaf
  And innocence was lost;
What shouts rose from the dæmon guard
  Who kept the fiery lakes below,
When the fair work of Heaven was marred
  By His eternal foe.

III.

The evening breeze on balmy wing
  Somewhile had cooled the noontide heat,
And the red sun was hastening
  Towards his nightly seat;
No more the new created pair,
  Watching his glorious descent,
Hymned forth their songs and tuneful prayer;
  In shame and fear they went,

To hide them in some distant shade
  From their offended Maker's sight;
Vain hope was theirs, if to evade
  Him, to Whom darkest night
Was as the sunny day.—Anon,
  They start to hear His voice well known,
Calling each terror stricken one
  In deep and chiding tone
To come before Him—who but he
  Who falls beneath his first offence,
Knows the heart-rending agony
  When early innocence
Is lost, and the first sin unmasked;
  The after-pangs grow weaker still,
As, day by day, the heart is tasked
  To do the tempter's will.
Weak plea they offered for their sin,
  His thought, perchance, whose flatteries
Had wrought such fearful change within
  Those bowers of Paradise,

Where now they tarry but to learn
  God's sentence given: " Dust ye are,
And unto dust shall ye return,
  Through toil, and want, and care."

NURSERY RHYMES.

I love these dear old songs, sweet thoughts they bring
Of old familiar scenes, and faces dear
Of loved ones now in churchyard slumbering,
Whose souls, we hope, are in a happier sphere;
My mother's tuneful voice seems echoing
With each remembered rhyme full in mine ear;
There sits my father full well pleased to hear
His little one catch up the jingling song
In mimicry. I cannot help this tear—
My heart will burst if I restrain it long,
Whilst its affections seeking eagerly
For beacons such as these, which they may hold
As guides along the track of memory,
To those the spirit loves above all price of gold.

SONNET.

I.

If thou art sad, seeing me sorrowful,
Then surely pity dwells thy breast within,
And pity, say they, is to love akin;
Oh! let me from that sweet hope solace cull:
And if such lovely kinsfolk do begin
To take possession of thy vacant heart,
Oh! do not banish them away again,
But let them hold an undivided part;
Or else then suffer love to have chief reign,
And I will be thy servant and thy slave;
Thine eyes look kindly, say not they belie
Their seeming nature, but their credit save,—
Oh! quench not sweetest pity from thine eye;
Love me for pity's sake,—and pity, else I die.

SONNET.

II.

Of all sweet flowers is Katherine the sweetest!
Of all bright gems is Katherine the brightest!
Alas, that of all moments those are fleetest
When spent with those in whom thou most delightest:
And Katherine to me is fairest, sweetest, dearest;
I cannot mete by words my soul's devotion;
Even the simple pleadings which thou hearest
Tremble upon my tongue with deep emotion,
Checking the stream within the heart's recesses
That floweth upwards to the lips, but meeting
With thy cold look which suddenly depresses
The rising tide, and sends it back repeating
(Yet only to itself) what it hath left unspoken,
And there it speaks aloud in eloquence unbroken.

SONNET.

III.

At last the swelling torrents in my soul
Are settling down again in stiller course;
It is not they have wasted all their force,
Or that the tides of love less deeply roll; .
No, no, the winter frost-winds of despair
Are binding them in adamantine chains
Of an eternal ice; a stillness reigns;
But it is one of desolation there:
The buoyancy of youth is gone from thence,
And with it Hope hath fled, whose sickly lamp
Grew paler, for the Autumn mists were dense,
As Summer vanished in his merry tramp:
To me no Spring will rise with genial beam
To melt again the frozen waters of life's stream.

SONNET.

IV.

Hope in my heart divideth sway with fear ;   .
Sometimes her sunny rays are rich and full,
And bids my sadder spirit take some cheer ;
Songs chaunteth she so sweetly, which do lull
The senses into many a pleasant trance,
And on her placid stream the life-bark glides ;
Then the dark shadows of fell doubt advance,
Obscuring the bright waters where Hope rides :
The low winds moan and chiller grows the air ;
Anon, Hope ceaseth her delusive chaunts,
And veils her stars ; then up from his dread haunts
Stride forth the dæmon spirits of despair,
Blasting the flowers around, and poisoning
The dews and springs which give them nourishing.

SONNET.

V.

I revel in the luxury of thought,
Which I may do, soaring from earth to heaven
Where e'er I list, and fetter'd down by nought
Of dull material form; oh! there is given
To some a power to lull themselves in dreams
Of pleasantrie, though all around them seems
Dark, tasteless, and brimful of torturing.—
How strange it is that things which have no link
Between themselves, yet to our memory bring
Scenes, forms most cherished,—sweetening,
Perchance, or else embittering the drink;
E'en here, where no associations seem to lie,
Things do present themselves, which shew my eye
One form so idolised, on which I love to think.

SONNET.

VI.

Alas! when we do love, how slight a thing
Will pour into our hearts the dregs of sorrow;
A word, a tone, a look, will often fling
A cloud upon those streams which only borrow
The sunshine from some momentary gleam
Which Hope sheds forth.   It is a mystery,
A woman's heart; for if awhile she seem
To let her tell-tale eyes unfold to thee
The secret of her heart, her tongue denies
What these confess; and thou art still in doubt
Or fear which check thy native energies,
And then each trifling circumstance without
Confirms the dark foreboding of the mind;—
The darkest overwhelming all Hope leaves behind.

SONNET.

VII.

'Tis true, imagination painteth ills,
But she hath pleasures too, and in her own
Warm climes she reareth many flowers alone,
From whose rich scented blossoms she distils
A charmed potion, which the spirit drinks;
And eftsoon in a pleasant trance she sinks,
Dreaming of all she loves; and sails along
As on a moonlit stream when sleeps the breeze ;
Nought heareth she, unless the heart's own song ;
Nought seeth she, but the fair sweet forms which
A golden sky fretted with stars of love ;
   please ;
Nought feeleth but a sweet tranquillity
And glad contentment, such as Heaven above
Will yield to those who rightly live and rightly die.

SONNET.

VIII.

I caught one glance of thee, and it awoke
The slumbering train of Hope, who for awhile
Fed high her meteor beams; and as she broke '
The midnight darkness in my soul, the smile
Of opening joys, as a fair summer's morn
Seemed dawning on me then.   I know not how
Such strange delusion seized me, but if thou
Hast ever loved, with hopes like mine forlorn,
Thou well may'st know what joy it is to meet
The idol saint of thought and memory
As I met thee.   I cannot tell thee why
Thine image takes its everlasting seat
Within my heart, but true it is, to thee
All thoughts will take their flight when I dare let them
    free.

SONNET.

IX.

Yes! in each reverie, thou art the theme—
In the fantastic visions of the sleep
Thou art the Fairy Queen with whom I seem
To hold sweet converse of the soul, and deep
Must be the impress thou hast made, to keep
The sway o'er those strange fancies; for they say,
'Tis then the spirit calleth to her side
Those whom she cherishes, and sails away
In her own native colours, on a tide
Sunn'd by her own bright hopes. Day may unwind
Such sweet enchantment, and dull earth uprear
Forms which may fill the eye and dim the mind;
It is but few of these she holdeth dear,
But secketh kindred spirits in another sphere.

SONNET.

X.

The seeds of Love are thrown into our hearts,—
We know not how, or why, by whom or whence
They come.   Sometimes a quick intelligence
Between the meeting eyes of each impart
The bosom thoughts of one unto the other,
Betraying sympathies with one another;
But if there be no mutual sympathy, ·
Love still is such a spiritual thing,
He will find light in dark uncertainty;
Rejoice when others would be sorrowing;
Light up Hope's torch when others would despair;
Feed on a look, and on a smile will thrive;
For years, perchance, he'll sleep in his deep lair
As if forgot or dead, and then he will revive.

SONNET.

XI.

If Memory were the vision of a dream
Alone, not of life's strong realities,
I could, perchance, put out the glimmering beam
Which ever and anon flits o'er the stream,
Tinted with Love and Hope's fond imageries;
But there's an essence in our minds defies
E'en the strong tyrant hand of circumstance,
Making a world within us which we prize
Beyond the world of our external glance;
And there our own and dearest home we form —
Gather the beings of our Spirit's choice,
To whom our pure affections deep and warm
Will fondly turn, and still despite the storm,
With those we most do love we seemingly rejoice.

SONNET.

XII.

Well were it now that I unstring my lyre,
Since I to move thy heart have sung in vain,
For bards of richer and more brilliant fire
Have, like myself, chaunted their lonely strain;
Murmur'd of broken hopes, and withered flowers;
Writhed under unrequited love; and striven
With feelings torn, and young affections driven
From dearest ties, and home's delightful bowers,
O'er disappointment's scathed and barren waste;
Yes! it is time to stop, there is within
My heart, as yet, a voice like one in haste
That telleth me of something yet to win;
But ah! my energies are faint and slow,
As manhood gathers up its weight of woe.

Henri V.

————◆————

RIGHT Royal Scion of a kingly line,
Well hast thou earned the laud of men and saints,
The sceptre of thy ancestors is thine,
Not by man's choice, but by the right divine;
And thou dost spurn to wield it by such feints
As this all shallow-minded age would praise
As politic and wise.   Far deeper ken
And purer faith directs thee still to raise
Thy proper hopes to Him, Who, not as men,
Sees the time's many changes, but doth guide
Events to their appointed ends; and when
The principles of truth and right shall ride
Triumphant over false expedience,
Then wilt thou take thine own, tho' the time be far
    hence.

"HO! EVERY ONE THAT THIRSTETH."

WHO may come
    And drink of the eternal river
Flowing in yon' celestial home
    Before the Almighty Giver?

Merciful Heaven!
    Thou wouldest all should come;—
To all the boon is freely given;
    Silver nor gold we need.

The Spirit and the Bride,
    And he that hears, say, 'come and taste;'
Shall he that thirsteth turn aside
    Whilst the stream runs to waste?

Which is the way?
    'Tis through yon' straight and narrow gate;
If few do find it, yet *all* may;
    Knock, enter ere it be too late.

K

THE tears of life grow cold
As manhood getteth old—
Hope shining in spring-time,
Also in summer's clime,
So warmeth with her beams
Those brief and passing streams
Falling in youth's gay hours,
That fair and scented flowers
Spring thick and fast and sweet
Beneath its dancing feet.

But when the Summer waneth,
Hope,—false one! ever feigneth
A sickness at the heart,
And sigheth to depart
For some yet untried soil,
Where she may have less toil
To raise her flowers again;
For thicker falls the rain,
When Summer is quite gone
And Winter draweth on.

The hearts which she hath left
Of her bright smile bereft,
Will see on their dull shore
Those flowers and fruits no more,
For as earth's sorrows press
Tears from each deep recess,
In icy streams these come
To the spirit's very home,
And in their chilly flood
Kill every young bud.

Flowers will no longer grow,
Or growing, will not blow,
Or blowing, will not bear,
So with'ring is the air;
And each remaining seed
Is washed away indeed,
Which might have lived to shed
Some halo o'er the bed,
Where all now rest in sleep,
Unbroken lone and deep.

TO A THRUSH SINGING ON NEW YEAR's DAY.

WHY art thou singing, little bird?
　　Winter is not departed,
Not a flower from the ground hath stirred,
　　Nor Spring on her gay course started.

The Sun cometh o'er the hill,
　　And danceth upon the river;
But the flowers and trees are leafless still,
　　And the cold winds make us shiver.

But sing, for thy life is brief,
　　And thy heart is free from sorrow;
Thou never dreamest of grief
　　That awaits thee on the morrow.

The song in thy little throat
　　Is the truest harmony;
The art of man hath not changed a note,—
　　It is full, it is clear, it is free.

Man when he wakes at dawn
  Toils thro' the day in sadness,
At night he may sit forlorn,
  And his dream may end in madness.

But thy heart is free from dread,
  And thy mates will ne'er forsake thee,
The bright red holly curtains thy head,
  And the songs of the rill awake thee—

Then warble on, sweet bird ;
  Thy mellow notes come o'er me
Like songs in my childhood heard,
  Ere the storm-clouds rolled before me.

IN

M. M. M.

PALE is thy cheek and brow,
    Oh very pale; those lips where hung
Sweet kisses, cold and white are now;
    All silent is the tongue
Which called to me in tones so kind,
    I ne'er again shall hear such spoken;
Sure, seven and thirty years will bind
    Ties not soon broken.

And yet how tranquilly and calm
    Thou waitest for the hour to part;
Hast Thou, in mercy, poured thy balm,
    Oh Father! in that lov'd one's heart?
Hear us, O King of Kings,
    And let thy blessed angels come
With Christ's salvation on their wings
    To bear her to her heavenly home.

Oh my mother !
Dread of this hour hath haunted me
Long, long ago, when I did smother
    The immediate poignancy,
Because I then could feel
    Thou still wer't near, and I could run
Into thy very arms, or kneel
    Whilst thou didst bless thy son ;
Aye, and my heart would leap
    With joy to hear thy voice the same
As when it lull'd me to my sleep
    Ere I could lisp thy name.

SONG.

SAY that I am a rover bold,
 And have sighed for many a flower;
That the tale of love has been often told,
 Or I changed it every hour;

I have broken vow nor faith with none,
 I have ne'er left one to weep; ·
If the flame of love was a lonely one,
 'Twas better to let it sleep,

Than to wear away life's summer years
 In a solitary dream,
Or to fill me a cup of bitter tears,
 When around was a glorious beam.

When I give my heart and another take,
 It will be a gift for ever;
The vows I plight I shall never break,
 The chain only death will sever.

But the gift must be to that one form
  In the sainted throng I cherish;
It hath hovered around in sheen and storm;
  Its memory ne'er will perish.

"THE END IS NOT YET."

NOTHER storm within thy fold
    And bitter foes without;
Thy sister hostile, as of old,
    Raising her trumpet-shout
To urge them on; sure, perils frown
    All darkly on thee now,
Soon must thou wear the martyr's crown
    Upon thy glorious brow.

Oh Bridegroom of the stricken Bride!
    Stretch forth thy mighty arm
In love, and let her safely hide
    Free from the threatened harm!
Oh pour into her bleeding wounds
    The balm of charity!
Soften these wild discordant sounds,
    And change the angry cry!

"UPON THE EARTH DISTRESS OF NATIONS."

WAIL is echoing in our ears
    From many a sister land;
The chief who erst in Heaven's own spheres
First marshall'd forth his angel peers
    In rebel league to stand,
Waves his dark wings triumphantly
    Whilst havoc and distress grow rife,
Deeming his own dominion nigh
    As wider spreads the strife.

Is this a time to be at ease
    Within our England's Isle?
Dare we to say, 'no sounds are these
    To chase away the smile
Upon each joyous brow, or stay
    The speculating scheme;
Let youth have out his holiday,
    Man reap his golden dream;'

Or say we, that our lamps are trimm'd,
　　Whene'er the Bridegroom calls,
His name and praise are ever hymn'd
　　In all our cots and halls ;
Righteous are we in thought and deed,
　　The purest faith we keep,
His favored children we, nor need
　　We fear to take our sleep ?

We flutter in broad sheen and glare,
　　We think it is the light,
Around our paths lie pit and snare
　　Scarce hidden from our sight ;
With ears all deaf, and mote in eye,
　　We hasten to the goal,
Blind leading blind, until the die
　　Is cast beyond control.

THE END.

LONDON :

PRINTED BY O. PHIPPS, RANELAGH STREET,

EATON SQUARE.